Art and Madness

Also by Anne Roiphe

Art and Madness

*A memoir of lust
without reason*

Anne Roiphe

NAN A. TALESE

Doubleday

New York London Toronto Sydney Auckland

All rights reserved. Published in the United States by
Nan A. Talese/Doubleday, a division of Random House, Inc.,
New York, and in Canada by Random House of Canada Limited,
Toronto.

www.nanatalese.com

Doubleday is a registered trademark of Random House, Inc.
Nan A. Talese and the colophon are trademarks of Random House, Inc.

Book design by Maria Carella
Jacket design by Emily Mahon
Frontispiece photo by Jonathan Bain

Library of Congress Cataloging-in-Publication Data
Roiphe, Anne Richardson, 1935–
    Art and madness : a memoir of lust without reason / Anne Roiphe. —
1st ed.
        p. cm.
    1. Roiphe, Anne Richardson, 1935– 2. Women authors, American —
20th century — Biography. I. Title.
    PS3568.O53Z46 2010
    813'.54 — dc22
    [B]   2010028051

ISBN 978-0-385-53164-1

PRINTED IN THE UNITED STATES OF AMERICA

10 9 8 7 6 5 4 3 2 1

First Edition

For Dr. Herman Roiphe

Foreword

by Katie Roiphe

There is a photograph of my mother on the back jacket of her first novel, her black hair cropped close, huge kohl-rimmed eyes, a daisy-print minidress, a cigarette dangling from her hand. She is very young and very beautiful and, one senses, the tiniest bit uncertain in this new role as author. The caption reads: "Anne Richardson is an active member of New York's young set." There are several aspects of this book jacket that are foreign to me: the name, the cigarette (she did not, in fact, know how to inhale), the young set. Who was my mother in her late twenties?

These were lost years. My mother, who has written comprehensively about every single period of her life, had never touched these years. She was one of the girls draped across the sofa at parties with Ed Doctorow, George Plimpton, Roy Lichtenstein, Terry Southern, Doc Humes, Jack Gelber, Norman Mailer, Peter Matthiessen, Larry Rivers, William Styron, and Arthur Miller. Decades later, when I would go to George Plimpton's house for *Paris Review* parties, they took place in the same brownstone by the river. Plimpton said to me once, "Those were wilder days when your mother was here." But what happened during those years? She wouldn't say. "Do I ask you what *you* did in your twenties?" was, I think, what she answered.

In those days, my mother was divorced from a brilliant, unsettled playwright and had a young child. She was living alone in an apartment at Eighty-sixth and Park Avenue, furnished with cheap rattan furniture, and had a black-and-white rabbit named Alouette, who was allowed to roam free through the apartment and ate the bindings off her French paperbacks.

In a sense, this book is the record of an idea as it moves through a life: the idea is the supreme and consuming importance of art. In her twenties my mother glorifies and reveres the artist in a way that is lost to us; a way that belongs to a world when book jackets said things like "Anne Richardson is an active member of New York's young set." The male artists and writers she knew were tremendously charismatic, seductive, and women, vast swaths of them apparently, were seduced. But my mother also witnessed the other side of the artistic endeavor, the dangerous, searing narcissistic regard that these men had for themselves: the cheating, the violence, the drugs and drink. And by the time she reaches her thirties and forties, she begins to feel differently: she is by this time a writer herself, and she approaches her work as a craft, in a deliberate, workmanlike way. She writes notes for her novels as she is shopping for cereal in the grocery store. She treats her work with all the romanticism of a factory worker off for a day on the assembly line. Gone the sense of the divine, gone the idea that any sacrifice is worth making for the art; and this book charts the slow and painful and interesting evolution of that change.

Recently, on a winter afternoon, I went with my mother to see a documentary on Doc Humes, the iconic novelist who had helped found *The Paris Review* with George Plimpton in Paris. I was lost in the appeal of their world, the drinks at sidewalk cafés, the stylish manic energy, the bookish glamour of it all. But I could sense next to me in the darkness some sort of opposing view. The Doc in the movie was lovable, quirky, magnetic, larger than life; but his daughter who had made the film hadn't captured the pain he lived in and conjured around him; she hadn't caught the viciousness of his physical attacks on his wife. I understood that my mother had known Doc Humes, but in exactly what capacity she hadn't told me.

Not long ago, I came across a letter my mother had written to Bernard Malamud, who would come to our yellow-shingled house in Nantucket for summers. "My love for you as a reader for a writer is as strong as any I have ever felt," she wrote. This line leaped out at me. How could your love for someone as a *reader* be as strong as any you ever felt? Somehow reading this now, remembering those summers in our yellow house, when my sister and I were sent out because Bern needed quiet to write, this reverence seems excessive, exotic. What did it mean, this serious, near-mystical devotion to writers, to the words on the page? Was there a time when people cared this much, when their intimacies were mingled to this extent with books?

Elizabeth Hardwick, herself married to a difficult poet, Robert Lowell, wrote about the women who surrounded the charismatic poets and writers of the period in an essay on Dylan Thomas. The "young ladies" she describes could easily have included my mother.

So powerful and beguiling was his image—the image of a self-destroying, dying young poet of genius, that he aroused the most sacrificial longings in women. He had lost his looks, he was disorganized to a degree beyond belief, he had a wife and children in genuine need, and young ladies felt that they had fallen in love with him. They fought over him; they nursed him while he retched and suffered and had delirium; they stayed up all night with him, and went to their jobs the next morning. One girl bought cowboy suits for his children. Enormous mental, moral and physical adjustments were necessary to those who would be the companions of this restless, frantic man. The girls were up to it—it was not a hardship but a privilege.

One of the fascinations of this document for me is that it tells the story of the girls who suffered for art, for the grandeur and silliness and exhilaration of the dream. The girls who devoted themselves to these men and, maybe more to the point, to the idea of these men. Why did they do it? What did it feel like?

On New Year's Day 2008, my mother sent me an e-mail about the party she went to the night before. She had run into Carol Southern, who was married to Terry Southern.

I saw Carol Southern who has been divorced from her husband Terry for at least forty years. Carol and I had been wives together, sat together at parties, shared a blanket on the beach with our children, at the time when the men were famous and drunk and raved and roared and had sex with other women and passed out at the end of evenings.

Tall, beautiful, Carol has been too many years alone. Her son, it was rumored, has struggled with drugs. I say to the man she is standing next to, "Carol and I have been through several fires together." Carol says, "I regret nothing. I would do it all over again." Her smile has now turned hard like the lights in the hospital corridor. "I regret nothing."

What did it mean to have the children of these difficult men? To watch that creative fire flame out, as it tended to, in someone else's very young life. To watch the illness, the hungers, replicated and reproduced. Can a poem, a play, a painting, a novel redeem or undo the damage done to a child caught in its creation? This was a question my mother spent many years answering, or it may be more precise to say that she lived the answer to it.

The culture, of course, has mirrored the shift in my mother's thinking, her retreat from the bewildering and seductive idol of the artist himself. The novelist most revered these days is the one who sells his novel as a screenplay to Hollywood for a lot of money. My sister's son is a sophomore at Harvard now. He is tall, blond, insanely confident. He said recently about one of his classes, "It's fine, I guess. But do you really *use* Tolstoy in your daily life?" He was interning at a hedge fund that summer.

Perhaps it is not sheer accident that the shift in my mother's thinking began with another man. My mother met my father, who was a doctor, at a party on the Upper West Side. She told me once about going to the Artists and Writers baseball game in the Hamptons with him before they were married. It is a big social event. It is a beautiful afternoon, warm, the gorgeous flat light in the soft trees calling out for someone to paint it. When they step out of the hot car, parked by the field, they hear a loud and bewildering caterwauling. There is a baby stuck in another car. The windows are closed, the doors are locked, and the baby is screaming. My father runs into the game, where the artists and writers are scenically clustered, some playing, some on the edge of the bleachers. He is shouting, "Who has left a baby in a car?" He is angry. It turns out that it was Larry Rivers's baby. Here the fever breaks. Next to a line of cars parked by a field in East Hampton. There was a baby locked in a car.

Art and Madness

1953: Fifth Avenue in New York City—I walk past the bronze statue of Atlas holding the world on his shoulders. The statue stands outside one of the Rockefeller Center buildings. The statue looms over the street, so does the building, a slab of concrete, an immense doorway, art deco rectangular windows, a monument to the engineering wonders of the 1930s. Atlas has blank eyes but his shining bronze muscles flex with the effort of supporting the steel girders of the giant planet resting on his broad back. Across the street the steps of St. Patrick's Cathedral lead to the thick steel doors, with stone arches above them going higher and higher. I see the arches repeating like stuttered words across the cathedral's face, points ending at the slope of the roof. Tourists, cameras, maps, white gloves, fedoras, hats with felt flowers on their brims enter and leave through the central portal. I am wondering if there is a fallout shelter in the basement of Rockefeller Center or under the nave of the cathedral. Where should I turn if I hear the roar of a plane, see the bomb descending toward me? I look at my shadow on the sidewalk. Will my shadow remain if I disintegrate in the hot flash of atomic matter?

I am not a phobic. I am not a prophet expecting God's judgment to arrive before tea and pastries are served under the palm fronds at the Plaza Hotel. I am not a follower of any sect, political or devout. I am an ordinary girl who has just purchased, at a store diagonally across the street from Atlas and a few steps from the cathedral, two pairs of Bermuda shorts to take to college, which will start in a few weeks. I have ordinary ambitions. I want to blow smoke rings into the dark as Louis Armstrong puffs his cheeks and blasts the air with sound. I want to watch the maraschino cherries float down in my whiskey sour. I would like to meet a boy who would give me his college scarf and one day perhaps a pin from his fraternity. I would like to take a boat to France. I would like to drink champagne with a man in a tuxedo who lights my cigarette with his hand cupped around a small burning flame. I would like to be happier than my mother and father.

I most certainly do not want the world to end before my eighteenth birthday. But I know the odds. I also know that geography was the name of my good fortune. I could have been a Jewish girl in Prague or Lodz or Vilna or hiding in Alsace or Amsterdam. I am a Jewish girl but one who was born in America. All Anne Frank and I shared was a common first name. But I understand perfectly well how little it would have mattered to the planet had I become ash and bone. Good luck was something that ran out, could be depended on to run out in time.

I had a pack of Lucky Strikes in my jacket pocket. I hadn't

been able to inhale without coughing but I was confident that I would learn. Everyone else did. I had a red lipstick in a gold case and a compact with a little fake ruby at the center of an embossed gold shell. I had good legs. I knew I had good legs and had no qualms about the male gaze, although I didn't call it that. I liked the male gaze. Reading the last issue of *The New Yorker* I had understood all the cartoons. Some I had to look at a long time but I had seen the joke even if I didn't laugh. I stared at the voluptuous women whose breasts Peter Arno drew dipping into their martini glasses. I got it, but what I got I couldn't have told you. Surely a person who understood the *New Yorker* cartoons was ready to join the fray. Surely a person who had read the Dorothy Parker short stories, all of them, was armed against the slings and arrows of misfortune. I had read Caesar on the Gallic Wars and Milton's *Paradise Lost* and John Steinbeck on dust and Walt Whitman on what I wasn't entirely sure. I had put God in the closet with my roller skates and was currently reading *Tender Is the Night*. Surely standing there on Fifth Avenue, my bobby socks sinking around my ankles, my blue-and-white saddle shoes as polished as they could be, I was ready to run the bulls in Pamplona should the opportunity arise. There I was at seventeen waiting for a man to carry me on his back, to support my world, to lift me up and never put me down. Ah, Atlas, pity you had no eyes to see me there waiting.

1946: *The New Yorker* had published John Hersey's article on Hiroshima. The issue contained only this one piece. It was sold out in a matter of hours. It was published as a book a year later. I read the book. I remember its maroon cover. It was slight but the weight of it was almost more than the mind could bear. It spoke of scorched skin and people pulverized into shadows that clung to the stones on the street after the bodies had evaporated. It spoke of pain that lasted and babies burned to the bone and radiation sickness that came days later and killed the dogs and the chickens and the mothers and fathers and priests, and of the pus and the wounds and the blindness and the unquenchable thirst of the survivors, most of whom were soon to die. I ate my breakfast. I went to school. I worried about whether my best friend was still my best friend. I continued to believe that even outside the Garden of Eden rivers ran pure and trees would give shade. I perfected my backhand and I wrote terrible poetry on the back of envelopes I stole from my mother's desk.

1962: My child is sleeping in her bed in the room next to mine. I am sleeping alone, my mother not a year gone from a melanoma, my father about to marry his longtime mistress, my brother in medical school, my disapproving brother, who tells me I too will die young of cancer: it's in the genes. And then there is my love, my new love, my child, who has only me, her father being drunk, disinterested, and probably, since it is now two in the morning, still at the bar of Elaine's, being brilliant and literary and wicked while smoking furiously and waiting for someone to pick up his tab, possibly Elaine herself. All this might have kept me awake, fearing for my life. But I sleep. I am

twenty-seven years old. The apartment was owned by my
mother. It is on Park Avenue, which she considered the right
place to live. Since my soon-to-be ex-husband was a playwright
and I with child, I lived near her, the economics ruled. But I
would have a different life from hers, I told myself.

A few months after my mother died, unable to speak, to
utter a sound, her eyes roaming around the room in search of a
cure no one could offer, my husband, Jack, left the apartment
and I was not surprised. He was not meant for ordinary tasks of
mortal days. Like Dracula he came to life at night, sleeping
during the day with the shades pulled against the light. Like a
tall, pale incarnation of a dark prince of a long-lost kingdom, he
survived on scotch and bourbon and cigarettes and German
philosophy and French paperbacks with the pungent smell of
glue in their bindings. When he woke his hands shook and his
eyes were red. I would have just returned from the playground,
the sand from the sandbox caught in the treads of my shoes.

A few weeks after he left I went to dinner at a friend's
apartment and her husband, a cardiologist, reached for me
across his new baby's bassinet and squeezed my breasts. "Meet
me for lunch," he murmured in my ear. I wouldn't. Then he
called and I agreed to meet him at the Algonquin Hotel. The
roundtable wits of the thirties and forties, the *New Yorker* writers,
the critics, had spent long hours flicking their long pointed
tongues at the passing scene, devouring the reputations, the
work, the ambitions of others. The Algonquin bar reeked of
wicked intelligence or its afterglow. I wanted to have a wicked
intelligence. I met the cardiologist there one afternoon. He

pressed his knee against mine. He explained that he loved his wife but that a man had the capacity for many encounters, pleasure was everywhere for the taking. In Madrid, in Rome, he said, every man had a girlfriend as well as a wife. Lily will never find out, he promised. "What I ask of you is commonplace," he added. "Don't be a puritan," he said to me. I didn't want to be a puritan. I ate the olive in my martini. I left the drink sitting on the table, daisy-colored in a cone-shaped glass. He had dark eyes with heavy lids. He had large hands. His black hair fell across his forehead, thick and curly. His wife was a painter. I had gone to their wedding. I had peered at his newborn son. I smoked three cigarettes, spilling ash all over the tablecloth, on my skirt. I promised to call him at his office, but I didn't. It wasn't virtue. I wasn't ready yet. I was practicing to break a commandment or two, the way a batter takes a few swings into the air before stepping up to the plate.

1963: The streetlights were dim in the dark below. An occasional car passed by. Far beneath the sidewalk the trains to Harlem and on to Westchester rumbled past in the blackness of their tunnel unheard, unheeded. The traffic lights changed from green to red and back again and the moon unseen passed overhead. I slept.

Then the phone rings. It is loud and I wake, suddenly. I answer. "Doc," the voice says. "It's Doc." Doc Humes, Harold Humes, best-selling novelist, designer of prefabricated houses, founder with George Plimpton and Peter Matthiessen of *The*

Paris Review, that Doc Humes was calling me at this unforgiving hour. "Yes," I say. My heart jumps. "What?" I ask. "My head was pushed into the mirror," he says. "I cut my face and there was blood all over my face." I am wide awake. "Are you bleeding now?" I ask. "That," he said, "is the terrible thing." "What?" I say. "When I looked in the mirror again I was not bleeding at all. I could see no cuts." "Then you're all right," I say. "It's the voice," he said. "What do you mean?" I ask. "The voice said to me, 'Work or I will kill you.' Then something pushed me into the mirror and when I pulled back I saw the cuts and the blood running down my face, the cuts that are gone now." "God," I say. "The voice says I have to write, but I can't. I will be dead by morning," he says. I say, "I'm coming, I'm coming down, give me the exact address." He does. He is staying in a cold-water flat on the still-unfashionable Lower East Side where my grandparents first lived when they landed on these shores. I hang up. I dress quickly, my bell-bottom jeans, my blue sweater with the holes in the elbow, and then I go to wake my child. She doesn't want to rise. I pull a sweater over her pajamas. I lift her in my arms. She wraps her small legs around my waist. My love for her is greater than all the seas that heave across the planet. Her head is buried in my shoulder. I take my purse. I go downstairs.

There are few taxis running along the avenue at this hour. I wave at the empty street with my free hand. Why did Doc call me? Why didn't he call his wife, the mother of his three young daughters? He had left his wife for the moment. He had perhaps forgotten her. He trusted me because I took him into my bed, whatever strange hour he came to the door. His bulky frame, his slightly protruding stomach, his wild eyes, pleasing me even when I knew the man was a snake charmer and I was a snake.

Artists were drinkers. Everyone knew that. Alcohol flooded through their veins the way the salt from the sea coated the lungs of fishermen out in a storm. Alcohol was the lubricant of genius, the secret ingredient that fertilized the words in the brain, words that would bring fame and fortune to those who could catch them and release them on the white page rolled into the typewriter. Artists had a way of losing their way as easily as the rest of us lost our keys or misplaced our pens. I believed in the drunkenness of artists the way I believed in the elephants' fondness for peanuts or the lust of cats for mice, the joy of earth for worms. The men needed to drink, needed to lift the heavy shadows that followed them about. They needed to chase away their fears of insignificance, their fears of being passed over, their old fears of the dark and what waited there: ignominy and the shame of failure. There were the old drunks like Hemingway and Fitzgerald and O'Hara and Ford Madox Ford, and then there were Nora and Nick Charles of *Thin Man* fame who sipped martinis day and night while solving murders. "Liquor is quicker," as Dorothy Parker said. Editors and writers went out to three-martini lunches and fell asleep at their desks in the late afternoon. Bars and clubs, ladies' luncheon spots all served drinks with olives and cherries and colored pink or green. But nevertheless in the afternoon the women sometimes threw up in the ladies' room and tipped the maid to clean away the evidence.

I believed that there would be no blue sky without the sun and there would be no books without scotch, no poems without rye. Alcohol was not a medical problem. It was the romantic grease of a dark story: the vampire love of my youth.

I believed that the most certain way to die was to live a normal life, a gray-flannel-suited life, a lonely crowded life, a life of commuter trains and country club luncheons. I believed that I was going to be a muse to a man of great talent and visit the bordellos of Morocco and sleep under the stars with the peasants of Franco's Spain. I was going to carry Hemingway's manuscript on trains that stopped in mountain towns with Gypsies singing on the platform. I was going to caress the forehead of the bedeviled and misunderstood F. Scott, while Zelda danced on tabletops when happiness had left her and madness had moved in. I believed that art, for me the art of the story, the written word, was worth dying for. I would have thrown myself under the wheels of an oncoming car if, as it moved forward, an undiscovered manuscript of Camus's had fluttered down to the ground. And I knew that night after night I would see empty glass after empty glass sit on the table as the men in the room called for refills, another, the one after that. I would watch them grow unsteady and make wild accusations and push each other. I would watch as the amber liquids pooled in the cells of the liver, turned the capillaries of the eyes red with eagerness, and made even very young hands shake as they waved in exaggerated gestures through smoke-filled rooms.

I carried with me into the West End Bar, the White Horse Tavern, a long list of things I would never do: I would never have my hair set in a beauty parlor. I would never move to a suburb and bake cakes or make casseroles. I would never go to a country club dance, although I did like the paper lanterns casting rainbow colors on the terrace. I would never invest in the stock market. I would never play canasta. I would never wear pearls. I would love like a nursling but I would never go near a man who had a portfolio or a set of golf clubs or a business or even a business suit. I would only love a wild thing. I didn't care if wild things tended to break hearts. I didn't care if they substituted scotch for breakfast cereal. I understood that wild things wrote suicide notes to the gods and were apt to show up three hours later than promised. I understood that art was long and life was short. This made artists Olympian and wives and girlfriends of artists had a great task: to pay bills, to supply meals, to keep fear of poverty at bay so creation could continue. Was this naked neurosis? Was it masochism in fancy dress? Was it innocence or corruption? Was it sweet or nasty or just plain stupid? I would take years to figure it out.

I wasn't a drinker myself. First of all, it all tasted terrible, even drowned in ginger ale, or diluted in soda, or swallowed quickly in a little glass. Second, it made me fall asleep and lose the thread of the conversation. I knew that women with their mascara running, with their lipstick smeared on their teeth, with their legs askew, with runs in their hose, tears and loud voices were undesirable, and to be undesirable was to make a fatal mistake. Also, long before the phrase became commonplace I had appointed myself the "designated driver." This was my trap but also my salvation.

I always had a soft spot in my heart for gangsters' dolls,
gunmen's molls. Cute ladies with low-cut silk dresses who always
got a raw deal no matter how well they passed the canapés
around, or lit a fellow's cigar, or sat on a lap and stroked a bald
head. I knew they had their thrills even if their cut of the action
was small.

A taxi comes. I place my sleeping child on the seat. I climb
in next to her. It is an expensive ride from Park Avenue to
Avenue A, but at this hour there are no other cars on the street
and we move quickly. My heart pounds. We arrive. I pull my
child out of the cab. She wakes and asks me where we are. I
stroke her hair. She puts her head down on my shoulder and
falls back asleep. I buzz the apartment. The door opens. I walk
up the four flights of urine-stained stairs. There is Doc waiting
for me on the landing. He looks like a man who has been
ruined, maimed. He stoops slightly. His face is unshaven but I
see no trace of a cut. I see no blood on the linoleum floor of the
apartment. His typewriter is on a small table in the kitchen that
also holds a bathtub. There is a mirror on the wall above the
table. "I was sitting here," and he shows me the worn armchair
in the corner. On the floor nearby sit empty bottles of beer:
many empty bottles of beer. "I couldn't work. I wasn't working,"
he says to me. His eyes hold mine. He is looking at me. There is
a tenderness in his look. He sees me. I think he really sees me.
He gently takes my child and places her on his bed and covers
her with his blanket. As he sets her down I hear more bottles
rattling on the floor under the bed. There is the smell of pot in
the air. The iron bars at the window that keep robbers from

entering cast shadows across the floor. The blanket he pulls over the child reeks of pot. He explains to me that he was sitting at his typewriter not writing a word when this furious loud roaring voice spoke. "This mirror has never been cracked," I say. "The mirror was splintered," he says. I don't argue the point.

I get a towel from the bathroom and wet it and wipe his forehead with it. He had published a best-selling book and another book equally heralded some ten years before and then there had been an interference, a static, a crumbling of his mind, as if an earthquake had dislodged the landscape, as if an ice age had frozen the gift he had been given and the words no longer came but the desire for them, the necessity of them remained. Everyone was waiting for his next book.

"I heard the voice," he says to me. "It will attack me again," he adds. "Stay with me," he says. "I will," I say. He is trembling. "In a few hours it will be morning," I say, "and I'll go with you to a hospital. You need a doctor." "I know I do," he says. We lie down together on the bed, the child tucked between us. He kisses the child so gently that tears come to my eyes. We wait together for the dawn. He does not sleep. He tells me he has not slept for days and days. The sky out the small window above the fire escape turns pink. I want to make tea but there are no supplies in the kitchen. In the half-size refrigerator another six-pack of beer waits. There is nothing to feed the child if she wakes. I say, "We are going, we are going to the hospital." He puts on his shoes. He puts on his coat. I try with my fingers to make his hair lie in one direction or another. He carries the child down the stairs. She wakes. "Are we going home?" she asks. "Yes," I answer. "I have a secret to tell Doc," she says. She whispers something into his ear. "What did she say?" I ask. "Our secret," he says to me. We stand on the street. We walk a few blocks. A cab comes around the corner. We get in. I give the address of the hospital. He is awake now. The cold air has rallied his spirits. "This book," he says, "is about aliens from another planet taking us over, they are taking us over." "In the book," I say. He says, "They are in the clouds." "In the book," I say. "You'll see," he says, "when I write the book." The cab moves uptown quickly. A few people are on their way to work. The sky is turning light blue. The day will be clear. The newsstands on the corners were opening their shutters. Trucks coming off the bridge into Manhattan were slowing us down. The child says, "Doc, are you coming home with me and Mommy?" "No," says Doc. "No," I say. We are three blocks from the hospital. The light turns red. The cab stops. Doc takes the child who is leaning against him and puts her in my lap and he opens the cab door and he is out in the street. "Bye," he says to me. He walks off, his open overcoat flapping in the wind. He walks in the opposite direction of the hospital. When the light changes and the cab moves forward I give the driver my address on Park Avenue. The child will be late for nursery school. I want a shower.

Doc Humes was an adulterer. His wife and children lived in a large apartment on the West Side. His children were beautiful and blond and very young, and his wife was calm and smart. Maybe she showed a little hardness (or was it exhaustion) around the corners of her eyes. She seemed like the perfect

Radcliffe girl caught in a Chinese dope den. I thought she was
less bewildered than cautious, more capable of survival than the
butterflies who surrounded her husband, butterflies like me. Her
voice when she spoke to her children was firm, faintly amused,
an intelligent irony behind the order she imposed. I thought she
was no one's fool. I did not think she was a poet or a girl who
dreamed of unicorns or painted on silk screens. She wasn't
trying to please or amuse. She was not anxious or uncertain.
Sometimes she was rude or perhaps frank. I was afraid of her the
way I had been of the mean girls I had known in school, the
ones who laughed at others who cared too much and were prone
to expose to the daylight matters best kept hidden from sight. I
saw that she had capable hands. I envied that. I thought she
must have been born to a wealthy family with old money and
raised with piano and tennis lessons. Actually she was the
daughter of immigrants who had made their way to America
through Shanghai just before the war. Her mother made dresses
for fine ladies. Doc Humes had all the signs and the blinding
aura of the aristocratic America she admired. Of course she
married him. It made her safe. It made her someone who wasn't
Jewish, who wasn't an immigrant. I understood that. Also he was
a writer, a famous writer, with famous writer friends and that
made him special, far more appealing than a banker or a lawyer.
He was that great creature we all admired, the outsider, the
inventor, the genius, one who could see what no one else could.
He was an artist and she would bear his children and wash his
clothes and care for him because there lay her own immortality,
there lay her own contribution to the great effort to speak the

truth, to shape the words, to write the novel that by existing would justify the human endeavor, an endeavor so clearly in need of justification. I know this because I felt it too, all of it.

Did she know that sometimes in his wanderings her husband rang my bell long after the hour when the doorman had fallen asleep on the couch in the lobby downstairs? If she knew she gave no sign. If she knew she didn't care. Out was out. In the night Doc Humes was out and it didn't matter where. I posed no threat. I could not steal him away from her. I was only one of the stops along his route. Sometimes I looked at her and wondered if the tinge of granite in her voice, a sound that seemed to keep sarcasm and pain in check, had always been with her or was it a sound that had arrived with the passions or lack of them in the marriage bed, or was it a sound that formed in the throat when she gave birth to her children and would never go away.

When I saw her at one party or another I smiled and we talked about children and schools. I didn't feel too guilty because I knew Doc Humes did not love me. He did not betray his wife with me. He only slept with me when the mood came upon him. His great restlessness brought him to my door sometimes. I would not deny a wandering lion with a thorn in his paw my best efforts. It was the bulk of him I wanted: the way he seemed to know everything or maybe it was everyone. And then there was the thorn in the paw, that distress of the mind so fierce and certain, so ruthless and still so caring. I didn't love the space-invader aliens he talked about. I knew that madness was assaulting him and I had no cure in the pockets of my shirt, in the cupboards of my apartment. What I had I gave him. It was scotch, or was it bourbon? It was large quantities of one or the other. But with every fiber of my being I wanted to hold him on my side of sanity and I thought I could. How I intended to do this I can't imagine. Did I have a plan? I doubt it.

Here is a moral problem. My ex-husband had not so much committed adultery as rode out into the night, pumped with nicotine, shining with watery red eyes, brain cells floating in alcohol, his words swinging like ropes across the room, tying all the pretty women into a group from which he picked one to follow home, night after night. He also roamed the streets looking for prostitutes, when he was drunk enough. He had explained to me that this was necessary for his well-being. He had to do this. His nerves required it. He did have to do it and I understood. But as I waited for him to come home in the early hours of the morning, I had come to feel that I was a fool, a lady-in-waiting in a court that didn't exist. If other women had my husband, I too could do as I pleased. This was not so much a moral choice as an abdication of morality. Fidelity seemed like a sucker's game. I had been betrayed by fairy-tale myths of happily ever after. My conscience ached but I ignored it.

My father, who did not love my mother, took to bed in downtown hotels, in uptown hotels, in apartments on the maid's day out, on the nanny's day out, on the cook's day out, my mother's friends, Dorothy, Sally, Helen, Honey, and others whose names I cannot remember. How did I know? I knew because my mother told me. Ice packs on her swollen eyes, a double scotch by the bedside, she told me. And I knew by the time I knew anything that the marriage vow was like the little boy's finger in the mythical dike, in the real world it wasn't going to hold. And so I understood, divorced lady that I now was, that I was a menace, a threat to someone else's hope for a reasonable ever after. I looked at Doc and detested him for what he would do to his wife. I also understood that I would not be an innocent bystander but, like Dorothy, Sally, Helen, and Honey, I would be both greedy and ashamed. I felt uneasy at how easy it was to become the other woman or one of the many other women. But then I believed or tried to believe that everyone should be free and every free act struck a blow against a world so cramped and sad that I could not endure it, would not pass it on to my daughter.

In other words I was unmoored, uncertain, and violated the only religious precept I really believed: Do unto others as you would have them do unto you. But those *untos* in the phrase marked it as ancient news from an ancient world that couldn't survive the things we knew, the things we did, the terrible monster that was mankind. It wasn't so much desire that led me as my intention not to live like a coward. I was determined to take what life would offer. I didn't want to be the only woman of my generation to hold to standards everyone else had long ago abandoned. I do not excuse this because of youth or anger or past history. I think that no one knew, was really sure, whether it was better to snatch what sex one could from passersby or to remain faithful to a love and miss the party, miss the circus and grow old and bitter. I wasn't sure what was right or wrong or if it mattered. I considered Simone de Beauvoir. She was not impressed by the Lord's commandments.

I had the morals of a four-year-old.

One night Doc's oldest daughter (was it Mellon?) was dancing in the matinee performance of *The Nutcracker*. Doc's wife and one of the younger girls had gone to see the performance. Doc was supposed to meet them at the ballet and afterward they were all planning to come to my house. I was at home with a friend or two. My child was running about the room throwing crayons at the bowl of peanuts on the table. They were landing everywhere. She wouldn't sleep. She wouldn't leave the room. I tried to bring her into her small bed but she resisted. She was exhausted, on the edge of a terrible tantrum, I wasn't sure what to do. Doc was at the door. He came into the room. You could feel his presence, the air was electric. He brought a kind of weight, a force came from him. He took my child by the hand. "It is time for bed," he said. He led her into her room. He stayed with her while the rest of us talked in the living room, half an hour, maybe more. He came out. "She's asleep," he said.

Then as had been arranged his wife and her two girls came. "You missed my performance," the older one said. "Why weren't you there?" she asked. "I couldn't come," he said. "I'm sorry," he added. He was sorry, I could tell. Doc's wife didn't look at him. "You know what I'm going to do," he said to the older one. "I'm going to buy you a horse." "A horse," she shouted and she threw her arms around him, all forgiven in the joy of the anticipated horse. His wife looked at him with cold eyes. "You cannot do that," she said. "You cannot promise her a horse. We have no place for a horse. We live in a city apartment. We have no money for a horse. You must not promise her a horse." The child looked at her father, now her face was about to crumple into tears. He said, "Don't worry, I'll work it out. She will have a horse." His wife turned away, her face pale and her lips tight. The rest of us in the room were embarrassed. This emotion was not meant to be seen in public. The youngest child in a party dress, all fancy for her evening at the ballet, began to pull on her hair ribbon. "Don't do that," snapped her mother. The child stopped. "We're going home," she said. She got the children's coats. "I'm staying," said Doc. "Just a while," he added. But it was four in the morning when he left, taking with him his cunning cruelty. As I closed the door on him and heard the elevator rising to my floor, I knew that whatever he was doing, he was not going home to his wife and children, not yet.

When he was gone I remembered how much I had wanted a horse as a child. A horse was out of the question. My mother was afraid of dogs and cats and we lived in the city and the upholstery was velvet and satin and the walls were painted turquoise and rose and gold sconces lit the hallway. But I had read every book about horses I could find. With tracing paper and a black pencil I had drawn the strong forelegs of great stallions, Man O' War and his friends. I had pages of pictures of horses that I had colored in with crayons and given names like River and Bear, names that spoke of pioneers moving West and Indian girls running free on the prairie. Why had I wanted a horse? I couldn't remember. Perhaps I had wanted to be a horse, a four-legged creature galloping free in the fields, a male horse, snorting white breath into the cold autumn air with the leaves falling and my own curly mane flying back in the wind. Perhaps I wanted a horse so I could bring it grain in a silver bucket, so I could brush its back, so I could lead it gently this way or that and it would obey my tug, because it knew I was its friend and master. Now I did have some friends but still no horse.

Back in the small town in Poland where my grandfather had lived as a boy before he came to the Lower East Side in the 1880s along with a flood of his kind, the Gentile folk had wide-backed horses with heavy hooves, pigs, chickens destined for early death, and shaggy flea-ridden dogs that drooled and snarled at passersby. The farmers smelled of stable and field. The town people had their own smells, dirty-sheet smells, onion smells, body-odor smells, tobacco smells, old-clothes smells, stale-bread smells, candles-burning smells, oil smells, dust-in-the-pages-of-prayer-books smells, wet-newspaper smells, potato-boiling smells. How strange then that the great-granddaughter of the shammash at the synagogue, the one responsible for gathering the ten men needed for prayer each morning, was now on Park Avenue, reading into the night about horses while her governess sat in the next room writing letters to her own family in a village miles outside of Munich. I too was at the campfire on the prairie as the wagons circled. Pa and Ma held the hands of the frightened children as the war-painted Indians rode single file past their encampment. My American root was bookish, fake, but dear to me nevertheless. It served to furnish the empty rooms of an uncertain self.

As I grew into young adulthood this self began to speak of "conformity," as if it were the great witch in the closet of one's childhood fears. Normal life beckoned with all the appeal of soiled bedsheets. I wanted to dance in the dark, cheek to cheek, with something dangerous, something that would make me feel alive. Frank Sinatra sang of love and crumpled his marriages as if they were napkins at the picnic table. People had gone to war and returned. Bravery was possible but not visible in my neighborhood. Great angry swirls of pain dripped and cut across the canvases of young men, young men who drank with their girlfriends in bars in Greenwich Village. Harlem was where we couldn't go. It was dangerous and we were hated there. But the music came from Harlem. If we listened, were we tourists or fakes? What was authentic? Was it the Frenchmen like Camus and Sartre or was it the poet Allen Ginsberg who at least knew that order wasn't order and sanity might not be a choice. The Rosenbergs were dead. There were gaily colored Negro jockeys in miniature outside the '21' Club. Toots Shor's kept the best tables for columnists and ballplayers. My mother lit her cigarettes with matches from the Stork Club. She spent eight hours a week at the hairdresser, curling, setting, pinning her hair and painting her nails that always chipped and required Band-Aids wrapped around the fingertips. The lights were on again in Paris, but how safe were we? She was always losing her white gloves in taxis.

If we spoke of the abyss in the familiar way that our grandparents had spoken of God, then had we lost our illusions or lost our way? I believed in the vast darkness of Sartre's universe and I believed that the streets of America were not so much paved with gold as with the ashes of human hopes. This did not prevent me from admiring Paul Robeson, who sang the ballad of America with a voice that challenged the heavens to keep its promises. It was hard to remember the absurdity of our petty existence even though that was the common word, that was the revealed truth, that was so true that it needed no further explanation. Nevertheless I kept feeling the warm flow from my womb, the desire for more children, the need to love someone, to grow things, to know more. Freud's unconscious interested me. Was I myself an abyss? Or was I an imposter abyss?

1945: Our synagogue, the one my mother attended on the High Holidays and the one my father never went to, that synagogue was like an old car loaded with treasures from the last home, strapped to the roof, bundled in the trunk, headed for the New World, speeding along toward distant places where the Torah pointer and the Talmud translations and the menorahs and the old Queen Esther costumes and the yarmulkes and the prayer shawls would seem like the white bones of a dead cow who had perished in a canyon way back and was hardly missed by the rest of the herd or its owner who had become a movie director in LA. In that synagogue I believed that God heard my prayers. I respected the written word, *Little Women, Anne of*

Green Gables, Peter Pan, Jane Eyre, The Secret Garden, Hans Brinker: or, The Silver Skates. I believed that God, fierce though He might be, commanding a father to sacrifice his only son, a fury of wild white hair blowing in the tornadoes, hurricanes that whipped through the sky, season after season, held the world in His great hands. Like the Lone Ranger, at the last minute He would ride in and alter the story. I also thought that He must like me, after all, what had I done, what had I lived long enough to do?

My mother is on the phone. Her scotch and soda sits on her night table. Her ashtray flows over onto the carpet below. There are lipstick smears on her pillowcase: red like blood. *Life* magazine lies open on my mother's bedspread. I see the photos of emaciated men and women in striped pajamas behind barbed wire. I see the crematoria. I see the trains.

There are those who say a person should get over the smoke of Auschwitz.

1963: A month or so after Doc's last visit: it is two thirty in the morning. The phone rings. I wake. It might be Doc. It must be Doc. He is in the neighborhood. He wants to come up. I am sure he wants to be in my bed and I am sure I want him there. I pick up the phone. There is silence and then a voice. It is not Doc. "I saw you today, with your little girl, on the street. You were wearing a red sweater with dots on it. I saw you," the voice said. "Who is this?" I say into the phone. "I met your ex-husband in a bar," the voice whispers into my ear. "I have been

watching you." I hang up. Why is he calling me? I am afraid and
so I turn on all the lights in the apartment except in my
daughter's room. I look out the window. I am on the eighth
floor. There is a doorman, a small leprechaun of a fellow with
dark circles under his eyes, an unlikely protector. I look out the
window. Perhaps I can see the man walking by. But he isn't in
sight. He couldn't be. There are no phone booths on Park
Avenue. I want to speak to Doc to tell him about the voice that
called but I have no number for him, except his home number.
I would call my ex-husband and see if he knows who this might
be. I would beg him not to give my name or phone number to
strangers at a bar. But this is the time of night when he is on the
prowl, maybe with a prostitute he has picked up somewhere or
maybe just talking and drinking and smoking in a bar, maybe he
is at Elaine's, but maybe not. I try to go back to sleep. I decide
never to wear my red sweater with the white dots again.

The next day it's raining. I wear my raincoat. I keep my head
down. I take my daughter to school and pick her up. Night
comes. My daughter wakes with a nightmare. She screams a
deep and terrible scream. I hold her in my arms. What terrible
shape was coming toward her? Why was I not able to protect her
in her dream? I take her to bed with me. She falls back asleep
and then the phone rings. "Your legs were bare," the voice says.
"I saw you crossing Eighty-fourth Street. Your hair was wet and I
couldn't see your eyes." "Who is this?" I shout. He hangs up. My
daughter has woken. She reaches for me. Her warm body leans
against mine. "You're cold," she says. I am cold. I should put her
back in her own bed. I don't.

The following night I lie in bed waiting. Perhaps the *he*, the *he* of the voice, won't call. But perhaps he will. I watch the hands on the clock. I think I should change my life. I should go to Appalachia and teach barefoot children the alphabet. I should go to Colorado and work as a waitress until someone who owns a ranch falls in love with me and my child and takes us to live high up in the mountains where fields of wildflowers spill down the paths. Instead I will take my child to her nursery school. I will walk the streets, the streets my mother walked in her Cuban heels, with her gold jewelry, with her lipstick dark and red.

I am waiting for something to happen to bring me life. I should go to Israel and plant tomatoes in long rows. I don't. The phone rings. It is the voice. "I saw your breasts today," it says. I slam down the phone. Fifteen minutes later it rings again. "The hair on your cunt must be black," he says. I say, "If you call again, I'll call the police." I hang up the phone. I wait. It rings again. I pick it up slowly. The voice says, "I'm lonely, talk to me. Tell me—" I stop him. "I'm calling the police now," I say. I hang up. I call my local precinct. It takes awhile. I am transferred from one desk to another but at last Detective Donald McBride is on the phone with me. His voice is deep, reassuring. He writes down what I say. He asks me about my ex-husband and I tell him he writes plays. Detective McBride played Hamlet in his high school play. We talk a little about Hamlet. Detective McBride went to Saint Ignatius Loyola School and became a cop like his father. I tell him I'm frightened because the voice had seen me and seen me with my child. Detective McBride likes the name of my daughter. "She'll be a fine woman, I'm sure," he says. I am calm in my bed. It is two thirty in the morning. I hear an occasional taxi going down Park Avenue. The sky is still dark, but perhaps not as dark as before I began talking to Detective McBride. I tell him the plot of Thomas Mann's *The Magic Mountain.*

The next night I fall asleep easily. I think I have heard the last of my unwanted caller. But the phone rings again. It's the voice. "I saw you—" he said. I interrupt him. "I called the police. They're going to trace your calls. You'll go to jail," I said. He hangs up. I go back to sleep. A few hours later the phone rings again. My heart beats too fast. My nightgown is soaking wet. I pick up the phone. It's Detective McBride. "I'm just checking on you," he says. "Everything all right?" I tell him. We talk about the mayor. We talk about the purge of the Jewish doctors in Russia in 1952, or rather I tell him about it and he tells me about the British campaign against the IRA. We both agree treachery is everywhere. We talk about Groucho Marx. He is a fan of Groucho Marx. He has the night shift, the dead-hours shift. He has a home and a family in the Bronx. I can see the sky turning the color of ice above the East River. I see the morning star isolated, still blinking like a drunk talking to himself after the bar has been emptied. "Good night," I say to Detective McBride. Soon my child will wake. Her dark hair will be tangled and damp, her eyes searching my face as if something new could be found there, something that would change everything for the better. I kiss her fingers, each one in turn. I wish she were a boy. I would fear for her less if she were a boy. On the way to school we pass the construction site down the block. The workers in hard hats are sitting in a row with their morning coffee in their hands, their backs against a series of barrels. I see their eyes on my legs. I see their eyes move up to my breasts. I don't mind. My skirt is very short. My body moves under my dress the way a body moves when it is being watched. The men whistle, they call out something. I can't make out the words but the intent is clear. My child turns around. Her face is red. "Leave my mother alone," she shouts. "Don't look at my mother." The men laugh. I pick her up in my arms. "It's all right," I say. "No," she says, "it's not. I hate them." I say nothing. I don't hate them. They don't have my phone number.

Along the street were cars and behind the men were steel beams and orange cones and toolboxes and above them came the noise of drills as heavy objects swung against thick cement columns. I wonder if the voice is watching. Let him watch, I think. I have my detective.

The following nights I do not hear from the voice. I have frightened the voice away. But night after night Detective McBride calls, just to find out how I am. We talk. "I'm sorry," I say, "to be taking up so much of your time." "My pleasure," says Detective McBride. "I'm lonely here. Talk to me," he says and I hear an urgency in his voice, a plea perhaps. And so it happened that I exchanged a lonely stranger for a lonely detective, all the while remaining lonely myself.

I arrive at my child's nursery school each morning at about the same time as a father with a boy in the same class. He is a psychiatrist. He has an office on the same block I live on. He has a younger son too who sometimes comes with him, carried in a sack on his back. He has a pale intense face. He is one of those men who are uneasy in their skin, not sure what to say, but when he looks at me I feel his interest. I wonder if he would like to take me to coffee after we have left our children at the classroom door. I imagine he must get back to his office to see patients. But one morning he stops me on the corner.

We sit together, knees touching in a crowded diner. He tells me that he has a closet full of paintings that he has been given by an artist patient who couldn't pay. He tells me that he likes to ski down mountains on paths that are forbidden. In the summer he goes to a cottage on the cape and swims miles out into the ocean. He owns a motorcycle. He drives it around the city. His wife won't let him take his boy to school on his bike. He tells me that he has a fantasy life that no one would expect. I am surprised. He looks so ordinary, so gray, so pale, so like a doctor with pens coming out of his jacket pocket. His face is curiously stiff as if held together by some kind of permanent glue. His wife, he says, is weeping with exhaustion. She says she can't take care of the children. I tell him my story. He puts his hand on mine. He does not have the hand of a daredevil. He has the hand of an accountant. We drink our coffee. It is time for his next patient. "Dr. Weisberg," I say, "thanks for the coffee." "Bill," he says, "call me Bill."

I could be the bacteria that caused the illness that would assault each member of the Weisberg family, including and most especially the little boys, one of whom was now building a castle with educationally approved blocks in the classroom where my daughter, my unruly daughter, was probably causing a disruption of some sort.

I thought of Dr. Weisberg's patients. No need for the choreographer to be a great dancer to do his job. I thought perhaps his bland outer manner might serve his patients well as a screen to project their souls on and to see themselves as they really are. But then I also thought I ought to stand outside his office building with a sign: "Dr. Weisberg is not to be trusted. Do not transfer anything to this man."

And so for the next few months I had a morning coffee date. Dr. Weisberg's schedule had changed to accommodate his time with me. We talked about our children. He told me about a patient of his who was afraid of ceilings falling down, his office ceiling in particular. My mother was always afraid of tunnels springing leaks, bridges breaking in two, elevators crashing through the roof, lightning piercing the window glass. I was afraid of nothing. I would not, however, ride on Dr. Weisberg's motorcycle. I had a child. My life was not my own to toss into the air like a coin—heads you win, tails you lose. We walked along Fifth Avenue, Dr. Bill and I, even as it grew cold and the wind blew in our faces and my nose turned red. He held my hand. Sooner or later I would have to invite him back to my apartment. It happened sooner. I remember my mornings with Bill Weisberg as a retreat from hope.

So we began to see each other rather the way some people go to the gym before they go to their office. He was not a passionate lover. He was not a joyous man. He was shy and sometimes he would sit there in his underwear and not move for moments on end until I reminded him that his next patient would be coming soon. When at twelve thirty I would pick up my child at the nursery school, his wife would be there with the younger one. We would say hello, smile at each other. She was bigger than I was, heavier, her dark eyes had circles under them. Her dresses were too long. She did not make Dr. Bill Weisberg happy. But then I expect no one could.

His smile was tight as if he were afraid to show his teeth. His hair was cut short as if he were in the military. He was clean, too clean. He washed his hands before he came to my bed and he washed them after he came to my bed. I knew he was sad. I was sad too but in a different way. I was having trouble thinking of things to talk about with him. His conversation was slow, deliberate, and sometimes his voice slipped into a monotone.

It happened during spring vacation. We were not meeting outside the classroom or in front of the red door at the school entrance as we usually did. We were not in the habit of calling each other. I did not miss him. Actually I did not think of him at all. Then it is late afternoon. I had talked with a friend in the playground who had a child my child's age. Her child was sitting on a bench coloring in a book. Mine was climbing up to the top of the bars and swinging there and then screaming in terror, calling to be helped down. My child speaks in long sentences. She remembers whole passages from books. Her eyes notice everything. She learns lyrics to songs in a flash. But she is restless, sobs deeply if I leave the room, sleeps fitfully, and won't do anything I ask. Her toys remain scattered across the floor. She won't put on her socks. She won't brush her teeth. There is a constant battle between us. I am baffled. I am tired. I think she will be an artist. I think she has words in her head like her father, flowing and flowing. The dark threatens her. The flush of the toilet frightens her. In her is a whirlwind of noise she cannot still. I want to calm her but I don't know how.

I return with my child from the playground. She is covered in sand and dirt and there is a scratch on her face that bleeds slightly. The phone rings. It is another mother from the class. "I thought you'd want to know," she says, "Dr. Weisberg was killed." I feel faint. I am silent. "It's on the news," she says. Bill Weisberg was riding his bike down Park Avenue when he apparently, for no reason, according to witnesses, swerved into a large oncoming garbage truck and the bike was smashed and he died before they could get him to the hospital. "My God," I say. "They're going to tell the children tomorrow in class," says the mother. Death, they're going to talk about death in the three-year-olds' class.

And so it was that Dr. Weisberg managed to break up with me, leave his wife, grieve his children, and silence his guilty conscience all in one decisive moment. Also there must have been something really awry with that man that I hadn't seen. Something that I had not noticed, perhaps out of cowardice, out of indifference, or out of selfishness. The picture in my mind of the motorcycle and the truck and the man on the street with broken bones and blood seeping over the lines in the crosswalk remains. I sent his wife a condolence note but I also avoided her eyes whenever I saw her. "Physician heal thyself," I wrote in my notebook. But then I tore out that page. Perhaps I should have been a better friend, not just a playmate. Perhaps I shouldn't have been a playmate at all. Before the school year ended his wife had moved away and her son was no longer in class with my child and it would have been easy enough to erase Dr. Weisberg from my memory. But I didn't.

1963: It is summertime. President Kennedy is still alive. I am living in a house in the Berkshires that I have rented with another family. They are good friends. The man is a voice coach, the woman is working for a union, and they have two children, a ten-year-old girl and a one-year-old boy. The house is old and rickety and smells of mold. It is furnished with faded rugs and stained cushions and there are spiderwebs in the corners, but the leaves from the trees brush against the windows. There is a pool and a dirt path and a view of nearby mountains from the upstairs bedrooms. I have an old car that overheats from time to time. My child jumps in the pool whenever she feels like it. She doesn't know how to swim and so I am always diving in after her, begging her not to go in without me. She has no fear of water, not deep water. She does have a fear of leaves. She screams if a leaf brushes against her arm. She jumps over them on the path. I discover that if I put some leaves in the pool she will not jump in. Each morning I sprinkle leaves across the turquoise-blue water. I am trying to write a book. I have a black notebook and I write in pencil so I can erase whenever I want.

Doc comes to visit. I don't know how long he will stay. We

have a small guest house on the property. I put him and his
satchel there. We go for a walk in the woods. He talks about the
smell of the pine, what smell means to human life, what smell
does for the mating rituals of animals. He is not a frail man. His
legs move fast and I have trouble keeping up. He talks all the
time and sometimes I can't hear him, or catch only part of the
sentence. My child is by the pool with my friend watching her.
My child did not want me to go off in the woods with Doc and
she clung to my body, and I had to pry off her small hands as
they dug into my neck. And now in the woods I wanted to be
back by the pool with my child. There were large black birds in
the high branches, a grating grinding noise came from above. I
put my hand on the moss growing on the tree trunk ahead of
me. I pause. I consider the possibility of snakes. Doc turns
around. "Take off your clothes," Doc says. I do what he says. I
look around for poison ivy or poison sumac. I don't see any.

Later we all have dinner. Doc talks about alternative galaxies
and life on other planets and the presence of the FBI in all our
lives, following us around, listening. He drank more than I
thought a man could before passing out. He didn't pass out. I
don't think he slept, not that night or the one after. His eyes
were red and he needed a shave but his voice was strong and
never stopped. My love did not soothe him. Every now and then
he opened a window or door looking outside for invaders,
intruders, enemies of the good.

That was the summer that a tall anxious actor in his forties
named Harry came to our rented house with his new love, a
young star of a very successful movie about two disturbed

teenagers. Harry had been in therapy for many years. Perhaps the therapy had given him a new chance. The girl was twenty-two years younger than he. She had large empty eyes. He seemed made of cardboard. The actor was ordinary but tall. The actor could not love, not even himself. The girl was too young to know that whatever she sought it was not in her actor who was on a first-name basis with many famous people, but was himself a star turning into another small black hole with an agent and a résumé that included a lot of summer stock. They joined our dinner table. My car overheated on the mountain road and I had to wait in the hot sun for hours until another car came and took me and the child into town. At night the mountains were black, hovering presences boding no good. Against the night sky the backs of bears, the tails of dragons, the tombs of giants appeared. It was no use telling myself that the mountains had no evil intentions, they didn't know I was there. I felt as I looked at them lumbering close by that the child and I were in danger, and I didn't know how to leave the rental, how to leave my friends, how to say what I saw in the mountains at dusk, at dawn, before daylight, when the scratching sound of small animals could be heard by the pool.

The actress girl had played a young patient at a mental hospital who had despaired of life. Now, in the mountains, she never smiled. She hardly spoke. Her olive skin, her graceful hands, her mouth settled in a puffy seal all made me wonder if in that movie was she acting or was she not. A school friend of hers arrives for a visit. The friend was the daughter of a famous psychoanalyst who had an office on Fifth Avenue and a fine

reputation until he began an affair with his patient, which
scandalized the community, the tight community of
psychoanalysts who had drawn a line that was meant to
keep patients safe from their therapists, therapists safe from their
patients. The scandal was all over town. The doctor had been
stripped of his honors, his teaching positions, his respect. The
patient had left her husband and the two lovers had gone to
another city. The daughter of the analyst whose mother was
now an object of pity was sunk in a fearsome lonely place,
sinfully abandoned. Her father's new wife, his ex-patient, was a
vibrant professor and years younger than the wife who had been
no more than a wife and a mother. Perhaps the old wife painted,
or cooked, or studied travel books and planned vacations.
Perhaps she was witty or played the piano, that I didn't know.
But her daughter that summer was like a wild dandelion picked
from the field, instantly pale, withered before her time.

So I was surprised when I saw Doc lead her off into the
woods for a walk. But then I wasn't surprised. I had not thought
he was mine, not even for the ten minutes he was mine. He had
an immense energy that if it had been colored would have
created tornadoes of purples and blues and reds above his head.
He would never be held by a single female body.

Years later I would hear a man say, "I was so angry I could
rape an ape." And I thought of Doc who didn't need to rape
anyone but whose every moment was suffused with something
that was born in the pit and would rise when the time was right
and roar out into the darkness where the rest of us were sleeping
and tear the trees from their roots and drink up the waters of

entire lakes and take for his own whatever maidens could be found.

When Doc returned with the girl from the woods her hand was held in his. Her movements were graceful, her color was pink. In her hair she had placed a few wild violets. Her long thin face seemed settled down, her eyes farther apart. Doc went to the cabinet where we kept the liquor and poured himself a drink. My child came running to sit on his lap and he took her up and played with her hair, pulling it in front of her eyes, and she patted his cheek. I couldn't get her off his lap to come to eat her dinner. He kept her with him and read her a story and the sun went down behind the mountains and the adults were sitting in the garden brushing the mosquitoes away and someone wanted to stage a performance of *Endgame* by Samuel Beckett off Broadway and someone else wanted to do Jean Genet's *The Maids* with all the characters in drag and the truth was no one had the money to stage anything. Someone asked why all the great writers are French and someone else said that it was the wine. Someone said that Samuel Beckett was Irish not French and that was true. Someone said Euripides was Greek and I said the author of Genesis was Jewish and as the bugs hummed and the candles burned down on the table we agreed that it wasn't nationality that made for good writing. What then? Luck.

At last in my bed I felt under my pillow for my notebook. Could I be lucky too?

IN THE MORNING the mountain air was cold. The smell of pine floated in the open window. I made Doc coffee. The child was still asleep. The kitchen had a large wooden table in its center. The child had crayoned on the table. I was trying to scrape off the color streaks. The wine bottles from the long evening before sat empty in the sink, on the counter, over by the cookbooks. The dishes had not been washed, tomato sauce turned dark and the strands of spaghetti stuck on plates waited for attention. Doc says, "I may be killed." I am not alarmed. He says, "I may be killed," the way other people say the stock market might drop or the daffodils in the garden might die in an early frost. "Be careful," I say because that's the polite thing to say. His bag is by his side. His eyes search every corner of the room as if the enemy lurked in the cupboards. I was going to drive him to the bus if I could start the car. He decides to walk. It's a long walk. "I want to walk," he says and disappears out the door. He doesn't look back. I wave but he doesn't see me wave. I believe in sexual freedom. I believe in personal freedom: in theory that is.

The child comes into the kitchen. She picks up the glass of milk I have put on the table and then, distracted, drops it on the floor. The glass breaks. I hold her in my arms. She cries, long sobs. "Don't cry," I say, "please please don't cry." How hard it must be to be this child whose mother is about to put her, still in her pajamas, in the car and race to the bus stop for a last goodbye.

I AM AT an off-Broadway theater watching a rehearsal. I know the theater director and his wife. She believes that society can be bettered if we elect good people and we need to be active in politics. We need to fight for our candidates, for an end to the war in Vietnam, for a society with equality for all. She is right. Somehow I am bored by all the details one must master along the road to justice. I don't care about councilmen and my mind drifts off when the conversation turns to whose fault it is that the poor grow poorer and the Negroes stay in their poor schools and the ugly dictators grab the scepter in distant and near places around the globe. The cold war has brought us bedfellows who are not just strange but are also lethal. But what is there to do about it? I suppose one could take to the bunkers, take to the metaphorical hills, join Martin Luther King in the streets, but I don't. My mind wanders when demonstrations are planned. Sometimes I forget the time or the date and miss them altogether and then I am ashamed. I want a better world. I just want someone else to create it. This is because I want to write a book. This is because I have imprinted in my mind, as if by Kafka's punishment machine, Beckett and Camus and think the universe is empty of meaning and so am I.

Later we are in the theater's basement and everyone is talking about the Kennedy assassination. We are all shaken. Who has done this? The Mafia? Richard Nixon, the FBI, the oil men of Texas? The Ku Klux Klan? The Russians? The Cubans? The bankers of Wall Street? Was it Lyndon Johnson? Could it really have been a lone lunatic with a gun? Word comes that Ruby has shot Oswald. Someone brings a small TV to a table and we watch. Oswald appears from behind a corner. A shadow approaches. A gun is raised. It happens again and again. Time is no longer moving forward. I want to go home to the child. I

want to go home to a person who would assure me that all will
be fine. In the end the good guys will win. I want to go home to
my bed. You can't be too paranoid, I think. Is someone planning
a coup? Is it a group of Nazi scientists that we rescued from the
bowels of Europe and made our own? I am thinking I really
ought to go to more meetings and demonstrations. But then I
think I can't, like the fabled little Dutch boy, save the country by
putting my finger in a dike. Even joining my finger to many
other fingers won't do it. The floodwaters have again breached
the levee.

How is it possible that we don't know if the man on the sixth
floor of the warehouse was helped by a person on the grassy
knoll or not? The power of myth to fill in for fact is amazing.

Are the stories I tell about my own life really true or have I
embroidered or omitted or lied to myself? Will we evolve one
day into organisms that don't care if something actually
happened or only seemed to happen or was just remembered
that way?

1952: I am memorizing the first chapter of *The Aeneid*.
Arma virumque cano. The words run through my dreams. I am
at a private school founded to provide the Rockefeller girls with
a respectable education. I have a date with a handsome boy
from Andover. I met him at Thanksgiving when I went to the
movies with him and a school friend who had a date with his
roommate, a fellow member of the tennis team. I talked about

Clifford Odets and the WPA and he talked about John Steinbeck and *The Grapes of Wrath*. We both had read John Dos Passos's *U.S.A.* and each of us wanted to write a book just like it. Now it is Christmas vacation and he wants to take me to Jimmy Ryan's, a jazz place on Fifty-second Street. The handsome boy is also the editor of the Andover yearbook. We had found ourselves on the front steps of the ice-cream place on Lexington Avenue. I had consumed two black-and-white sodas. He had a cherry coke. He was smoking a Camel cigarette. He inhaled and exhaled like Nick Charles in *The Thin Man*. He had a silver cigarette case in the pocket of his camel-hair coat. He told me that he was a Socialist. He told me I should read Trotsky. I said I would. At my girls' school we wore the wool scarves of boys from Andover (crimson and white), Exeter (blue and white), Taft, and Choate. Do I have the colors right or have they mixed and blended with the years? We were invited to an occasional weekend at those schools. The invitation was paid for with kisses and promises. A collection of scarves gave a girl a certain aura, a sophistication, a flair. A lack of scarves was a sign of neglect and rejection. I wanted an Andover scarf for my collection. I was interested in Karl Marx and Descartes. I believed that Caesar had betrayed Vercingetorix by bringing him back to Rome in chains after promising him dignity in defeat. I hated Caesar and swore to my Latin teacher that I would never forgive him. I believed that Jackie Robinson was a leader in search of followers. I would have followed him into the desert and across the Red Sea. I also had written a letter to William Saroyan to thank him for his understanding of the lonely like me. My date and I had both read *The Grapes of Wrath*. I knew there was sex in the book but I wasn't entirely clear about who did what with whom. I did not confide this to my date. I knew the world was not a safe place for innocents or dreamers or visionaries or Jews. I had very little interest in safety.

A cold December night. He came to my apartment to pick me up. I wore my pearls and my black cocktail dress with the rhinestones sparkling at the neckline. I wore my camel-hair coat and a charm bracelet. My favorite charm was a tiny golden baby carriage with tiny wheels that turned. We stood in a long line waiting to get into Jimmy Ryan's. I shivered in the cold. My legs were almost numb. My corset cut into my stomach and the straps that held up my stockings were making deep marks in my thighs. At last, after a quick lie about our ages we were allowed in. Small tables with candlelight greeted us. A blue-and-silver wall shined from the stage lights. The band was up on the stage. Smoke swirled in rising and falling waves about the heads of waiters and musicians. The doors to my childhood slammed shut behind me. Something in my body surged and tingled in a way that it never had before. The band played "When the Saints Go Marching In," the trumpet wailed, the bass carried the theme, the drummer riffed. I ordered a rye and ginger ale. I ate the cherry from my date's manhattan. I ate the olive from the martini that the boy at the table behind us offered me because I was staring at it, just sitting ignored in his glass. There was a break. The musicians left the stage. My date said, I have something important to show you. He pulled a letter out of his pocket. As the editor of the Andover yearbook he had written to

J. D. Salinger and asked him to write an introduction. Everyone had read *The Catcher in the Rye*. I had read it about eight times. We all thought it was about not conforming, not believing all the stuff the adults told you, we thought it was about rebellion and truth and trying to be honest. I had not understood that a male teacher had made a pass at Holden. I had not understood that the point of the book was not so much Holden's anger at the world but his great grief at his brother's death. I had not understood that the country itself was mourning without mourning the dead of the war, the sons and fathers who would never come home. I did not see that the hypocrisy that Holden so despised was caused by a mass turning away from the dead, from their memory. But I loved Holden. I wanted Holden, or some Holden substitute, to love me, to take me away to the mountains and live with me in a shack. And here I am at Jimmy Ryan's and my date has in his hand a letter from Salinger himself.

The letter said, "Because I am not a student at your school I cannot write the introduction to your yearbook but I suggest that on the train home at Christmas vacation you walk through the cars until you find a small boy with his nose running, attempting to get his suitcase up on the rack. He will be sitting alone. Ask him to write your introduction. He will know what to say." The letter was signed by J. D. Salinger.

The cigarette smoke made my eyes tear. When we returned to the front door of my apartment, before letting myself in with my key that I kept on a pink ribbon in my velvet purse, I let Bill kiss me until his face was covered with lipstick. I let him put his hands on my breasts. I didn't let him do anything else because I knew that if I did he would talk about me. At my door he became not a handsome date who had listened to "Somebody to Watch Over Me" and put his hand on my hand in a promising sort of way but a predator, not the knight in shining armor but the opposing knight who would defeat my queen in the most important game of my life. "No one will marry you if you are not a virgin," said my mother. "You will be spoiled goods." I did not want to be spoiled goods. In fact I didn't want to be any kind of goods: piece or otherwise.

My mother told me never to sign any petition no matter who asked me because my signature could come back to ruin my life one day. My father dressed each morning in his perfect blue suit and his proper tie. He put on his fedora and his gray suede gloves and he carried a monogrammed briefcase off to work. At night he ground his teeth, put cold compresses on his migraine-suffering head, and released waves of sound, jaw-snapping, teeth-bared, bloodied sound, as my mother wept and wept and put compresses on her eyes that should have stopped the swelling of the lids but didn't. She read *The New Yorker,* played solitaire on her bedcovers, and drank scotch and water, one and then another. My father spent the early evening at his club, a club that admitted women no farther than the outside lobby, where the cold winter air froze the toes of the wives waiting for their men to come join them for the theater. There my father was playing squash, talking golf, and trading stock tips, as often and as long as possible. The decorator had done our apartment just like all the others in my mother's crowd, turquoise-and-red-velvet wallpaper and chinoiserie and gold lamps and pale blue carpets and mirrors on the walls in every corner. The cook listened to the soap operas on her little radio in her small room behind the kitchen. The maid in the next-door room wrote letters home to her family in County Cork. My mother did crossword puzzles, took beauty cures for dry skin, and removed unwanted hair. No one believed in God. No one was looking for God. No one was waiting for the revolution. The great thing was that everything should seem all right. Everything seemed all right. Perhaps because we were American Jews we were just grateful that no one was planning to transport us to our deaths. But no one said that. What they said was that the Rosenbergs deserved to die.

I believed along with Holden that everyone was phony, including me. My tenth-grade English teacher was a large-boned woman who wore mannish suits and men's shoes. She wore no makeup, a decision that would be common in another ten years but spoke volumes at the time. She hovered like an angel above Odysseus, above Beowulf, above the Fool in *King Lear*. But sometime before the Thanksgiving vacation she began to talk of something else. She told us that the FBI was listening to her in the classroom and we should be careful what we said. She told us that certain governmental agents spoke to her through her radio and accused her of disloyalty to the United States. She said that the Scottish headmistress of the school was a spy for the FBI. She said that some mysterious *they* had put metal into her teeth that could record what she said. She had deep shadows under her eyes. Her hair was unwashed and hung down on her neck in greasy snarls. She sometimes stopped talking in class altogether, mopping sweat from her pale face, while we sat in embarrassed silence. I loved her with that fierce love of a girl for a woman who knows what the words on the page really mean. One day she didn't come to class. Someone said she had been carted off to the loony bin. Someone made fun of her shoes.

IN OUR BLUE tunic uniforms with white blouses underneath and blue bloomers, we hid under our desks with one arm flung across the face to protect the eyes from radiation and the other arm we held behind our necks to save our spines from falling glass and flying objects. We did this at least twice a month when an alarm bell would ring in the middle of class, telling us that we were in an atomic warfare drill. At least we hoped it was a drill. It became routine enough. Although each time I would see myself walking through the rubble of the city streets, trying to find my mother. I would imagine the burned bodies and the broken windows and the wind that was poison and would burn the skin that would fall off my arm. We were in a cold war that could turn hot. Under my desk waiting for the all-clear bell I would, each time, conjugate the French, *je suis, tu suis, il suit, nous suivons*, over and over. This silent chant was surprisingly effective. The bomb never fell.

In the gym I pass and push and run and dribble and shoot and careen into the walls and sweat runs off my face and down my uniform blouse and I am happy. My socks drip down my ankles, my hair escapes its comb. No one else on the team cares that we win the way I care but that is all right, my caring is enough for all of us.

1962: Doc Humes says I should be firmer with my child. "Shout at her," he says. My friend Wendy says, "You must sit down at the table with her and don't feed her out of cans. Set the table and put her food on a plate. Create order around her." I try. My friend Fran from the playground has a daughter the same age as mine. She is a clinical social worker. We are standing on Lexington Avenue in front of the 92nd Street Y. We have taken the girls for a dance class. Her child had done what all the other children did. Mine had run in circles, talked all the time, and refused to get in line. Fran says, "Your child is going to have trouble. She can't concentrate. She's too wild." I am furious with her. The little girls are now in their strollers. Mine is shredding a napkin and bouncing in her seat. Hers is eating a cookie. My child is so clever, I think to myself. My child is an artist, I say to myself. But I hear Fran. I know she is saying something true. "Go and get her tested," she says. I have a sharp pain in my stomach. I have harmed the one person in the world who I most love. Men go to war and test themselves. They battle in the law courts, or on the operating table, or in boardrooms, or in front of typewriters, or with canvases spread in front of them.

All I wanted was to make this child a person who would feel and think and love. Had I already failed, done something wrong? The wrong was in giving her a father who would leave and not remember to come and visit, not remember to call. Divorce could scar a child. Perhaps I was too weak, too uncertain myself. Bettelheim, Spock, the experts all said it was up to the mother. What kind of a mother monster was I? I leave my friend and her daughter on the corner where we usually separated. When we reach home I call the Child Development Center and ask to make an appointment to have my daughter tested. I say this very calmly but I do not feel calm. I am placed on a waiting list and receive an appointment nine months, five thousand and two temper tantrums later, a week before the child's third birthday.

By the time the appointment was near I knew something was wrong. My brilliant child who had spoken in long sentences before the age of one was afflicted with some damage whose name I did not know, something I had done from the toxic core of my soul. But perhaps they could fix it at the Child Development Center.

1953: I am a freshman at Smith College. I am in a large dormitory. I am stunned. The boys from Dartmouth and Yale, from Harvard and Amherst come by on Friday night and walk through our lounge where we sit pretending not to notice the looks we are getting, the examination of our faces and our legs. After a while a boy would come up to a girl, ask her name, and invite her out for a drink with his friends. She would introduce the boy to the housemother, who sat primly at one end of the room serving tea from china cups with rosebuds climbing up the sides, and quickly fetch her coat and walk off into the night. A car would be waiting. When all the boys of a particular group had a selected girl in tow the group would leave the campus for a bar, for a hamburger, for a little petting on a dark road. This waiting to be chosen was frightening. My stomach would turn over and over and the animated smile on my face as I talked to whatever girl I was sitting near never changed. What if I was left over, found unattractive, spending the evening with the other rejected ones, too fat, too ugly, too strange, too bookish or foreign, too Asian, a Negro, a girl with heavy braces still on her teeth. I was chosen. I knew how to look at a boy and then look away as if I didn't care. I knew that I needed to put a boy at ease instantly. They were shy. They worried you might say no. They had their own bad thoughts that they hoped were not showing through their button-down shirts, their jackets, their ties. In the back of the car I always knew just how far to go and how far not to go. It was not so much a pleasure as a kind of bullfight, one in which the bull was able to survive for next week's encounter.

At Smith that year, 1953, the girls were all knitting argyle socks for their boyfriends. The socks required many small needles from which balls of red, blue, yellow, gray yarn dangled. During class the little needles would drop and roll down the floor, rattle, rattle, until coming to a stop beneath the lecturer's podium. Often I lost the professor's words in the clatter of needles.

In my dormitory there were seventy-five copies of *The New York Times* delivered to a front table each morning. This was a bequest of an alumna. Each morning I would take a copy of the *Times* and each afternoon I would look at the table on which the remaining seventy-four copies still sat until the housemaid threw them away. Joe McCarthy was ranting and pulling lists of Commies, saboteurs, and enemies of the state out of his pocket and roaring into microphones the names of the traitors. A few ardent anti-Communists had started a campaign to get two art professors fired. They were gay, perhaps; they were liberal, most likely. They were probably not threats to the state but letters went out asking the alumnae to withhold contributions to the college until the traitors were fired. The president of the college was resisting the pressure. One day at chapel he spoke of the rights of the accused and he got angry and with a thunderous boom he slammed shut the large Bible on the podium before him. A campaign was started to get him fired because of his disrespect for the Bible. There was a naming-of-names issue, who would and who wouldn't. There was a fear among the least-political among us that we might be snared, ruined by a friendship with a fellow traveler. So soon after the war we had fought for our free way of life, thinking what you will and saying what you wanted came at an increasing risk to your future job possibilities, to your relatives' job possibilities. There was a probably ridiculous belief that J. Edgar Hoover was everywhere with listening devices and it was said that his moles attended anything that might appear to be a political gathering. Riding

my bike on the path, weaving between the sea of girls in
Bermuda shorts and cashmere sweaters, I felt the breath of the
government turning the fall wind colder and colder on my neck.

Many of my dorm mates wore small gold pins, Greek letters,
on their cashmere sweaters above their left breast. These girls
were pinned, which was kind of engaged to be married, to boys
from various fraternities at the male institutions. It was a sign of
victory to sport one of those pins. It was a sign of a future
assured. I wanted a pin. I wanted to go to Dartmouth for the
winter weekend and see the fabled ice sculptures. I wanted to go
to Harvard and listen to the discussions of politics and law I
assumed were taking place inside of the red-brick dormitories
with their high fireplaces and male smell of sweat and smoke
and beer. I read Aldous Huxley's *The Doors of Perception* and
decided that LSD might be the answer to the sense of
suffocation I was beginning to feel, the way my teeth ground at
the sound of the falling needles. I went to the infirmary and
asked the nurse if she might obtain some LSD so we, the worthy
students of Smith College, could see for ourselves if the voyage
it provided was soul altering. I read her some passages from the
Huxley book. She said she doubted she could obtain the drug.
She offered me aspirin.

I combed my hair over my eyes. I biked on the paths to class
unseeing, occasionally smashing into a lamppost or another
biker. I ate jelly doughnuts by the dozens. For several months I
dated a boy from Yale whose father was the editor of a well-
known Southern newspaper. He was a competitive swimmer. He
had the dark sad eyes of a seal. He sent me poems about

drowned butterflies. Poems I did not understand but wanted to most earnestly. Then he went into the hospital with a nervous breakdown, left college, and sent me several letters with blank pages enclosed.

I transferred to Sarah Lawrence after my freshman year. I never completed a single pair of argyle socks.

The following year, 1955, the year that Sylvia Plath graduated from Smith College, the speaker at the commencement was Adlai Stevenson. He said, "In modern America the home is not the boundary of a woman's life. There are outside activities aplenty. But even more important is the fact, surely, that what you have learned and can learn will fit you for the primary task of making homes and whole human beings in whom the rational values of freedom, tolerance, charity and free inquiry can take root." The audience of assembled parents, brothers and sisters, graduates and their boyfriends applauded. Could Sylvia Plath have joined the approving crowd? I'm sure she did.

1958: A year after my graduation from Sarah Lawrence, when I was twenty-two, a married woman, my husband and I had returned to New York and he was writing a play. I was working to support him. It was not easy to get a job. My typing was mediocre despite the secretarial course my mother had paid for. My experience was nil. The magazines where I wanted to work would tell me that the only openings were in their mail rooms and because I had a college degree I was overqualified. I was underqualified for everything else.

At last I found a job at a small public relations firm answering their phone and sitting at their front desk. The job paid about $65 a week, which when added to by pawning our wedding presents was almost enough—although the strain of my husband's bar needs often brought me to my mother for help, just a few dollars for this or that. In the evenings after work I would sit down at the typewriter and type in clean copy the words of Jack's playscript. I used two carbons. My typing improved.

The public relations firm had a major client. It was Governor Rockefeller's fallout-shelter program. His office was encouraging New Yorkers from Albany to New York City and the suburbs to buy and build and stock fallout shelters in case of atomic attack. These shelters were dug into the suburban gardens and had steel doors and flashlights and water jugs and rations enough for a family of four for six weeks, time enough for the first blast of radiation to have lost its lethal strength. I forget how people were supposed to breathe but there must have been a way.

I wondered if fallout shelters would have saved lives in Hiroshima. I wondered when the bomb fell on Columbus Circle what my last thoughts would be. I considered rehearsing a last thought so that I wouldn't be caught without one when the time came. There were dummy shelters set up in the governor's office showing mannequin children playing Monopoly on the shelter floor. There were radios and telegraph sets and packages of cereal on the table. My firm was organizing meetings with all the organizations around the state to present the shelter and its virtues to the public. We held meetings with the Elks and the Lions Club in all the big cities. We went to the big churches and our presentation was featured at county fairs and at city halls. I handed out leaflets, answered questions about dried cereal and radio signals. The shelters were less expensive than a new car and could save the lives of all the members of a family. We always sold a good number and had the names and addresses of other potential customers eager to assure their survival in a burning radiated world. There were skeptics of course. There was a lot of talk about buying a gun to go with your shelter in order to keep your neighbor out if the time came because you would need your food and water for yourself. There were some on the political left who felt the entire campaign was intended to frighten the public.

In the home office on Fifty-fifth Street just off Madison Avenue I answered the phone, talked to anyone who asked questions about the shelter, and helped arrange the luncheons and the evening meetings. I mailed out invitations. I licked the stamps. I ran back and forth to the governor's office with lists of organizations, with names of people we had contacted. On one of those visits I was in the anteroom waiting for a secretary to come and take the package that was in my hand, and I saw a large chart on a poster. It was a map of New York State. There was a red circle drawn around the statue of Columbus in New York City and then there was a heavy red line that ran across the map just outside of Albany. There was a blue circle around the state capitol building in Albany and a thick blue line that ran just outside of Tarrytown. The information at the bottom of the map told me that the red line represented the bomb falling on Columbus Circle, in which case the first time the fallout shelters would be guaranteed effective would be past the thick red line outside of Albany. All the people living in between, the old, the young, the ones with shelters, the ones without, would probably be incinerated immediately or killed by radiation winds in the following days. The blue circle around the capitol building in Albany represented what would happen if the bomb missed New York City and fell on Albany. In which case the first time the fallout shelters might be lifesaving would be somewhere on the borders of the near suburbs: Tarrytown, Scarsdale, White Plains. That left the bulk of the population helpless as the atomic dawn arrived. But we were selling these shelters all over the state. We had meetings in the middle cities, in Buffalo and Rochester and the towns of Pawling and New Paltz. People were paying money for a protection that had only the slimmest of chances of saving them. When the secretary emerged from her office I asked her about this. She said, "We don't know where the bomb will fall so we should try to protect everyone." That was reasonable. But I knew that all the promises we were making to the Sisters of the Star and the librarians of Cooperstown, the Rotary clubs and the mayors of towns too small to have names I remember, were never to be kept.

Ants and spiders, ferns and pines, armadillos and pink-assed monkeys, whales, mice, termites, bacteria and viruses, dogs and cows and me and mine—we might all be incinerated. Silence in the shell of a city, no baby crying, no car honking, no ambulance shrieking, no lovers moaning, no drunks throwing up in the alley, no lights, nothing but wind and rain and snow in its season and rust and a rattling of open doors and carcass smell. It was a possibility like a brain tumor or a scorpion bite.

In the evening when I returned from work, just as I was sitting down to the desk to type his day's work, my husband would be preparing to go out. He would have emptied my purse of any dollar bills there. He would have dressed in his best jacket and tie, and his hair, his beautiful black hair would be sloping over his high forehead. His long fingers would be waving in impatience to leave. We had a television. It was a black-and-white. It showed Western dramas, good guys versus bad ones, cattlemen versus farmers, outlaws versus sheriffs. In the late-night hours as I tried to stay awake waiting for his return I would curl up on a chair in front of the television. We both had the same ambitions for his success. We both thought he was a genius. Perhaps I believed it more than he. We both had the same bibles. These were Samuel Beckett, Marcel Proust, Jean-Paul Sartre, Thomas Mann, André Gide. He would have included Céline. I could not because of the anti-Semitism. He wished I were taller, blonder, slimmer. He would point to the cover of *Vogue*. "If she's a woman," he would say, "what are you?" I thought he was perfect. I wondered how women married men who did not want to be writers, men who would be ordinary, pay bills, hold down jobs, think whatever everyone else thought, who would not make something new, write a play, a novel, paint a canvas. What were those women doing with their lives? It seemed so sad to live without a reach to the glorious, to be silent while the world passed by. I thought that women who had married doctors and lawyers, stockbrokers and dealers in real estate or politicians had settled, had lost hope.

I was waiting for a wisp of truth, a feather's brush of beauty, a moment of insight. My desire was fierce. My husband wanted fame. He wanted to be as famous as Keats. "If I am not as famous as Keats by the age of twenty-six," he said to me, "I will kill myself." In his twenty-sixth year, Keats died. Bravado, I thought. But I understood. He wanted to be a giant among men. I wanted that for him. I wanted to be married to Keats, a Keats who had a chance to survive tuberculosis and grow into a much honored old age or even a Keats who would die young but be remembered forever.

1956: I am sitting on a barstool in the West End Bar on 114th Street just outside the gates of Columbia University. I am a Sarah Lawrence student but I have driven down in my Chevy convertible from Bronxville to sit at the bar and look at the writers who gather there. I have heard that writers live in that place, drape themselves around the horseshoe-shaped mahogany bar and eat pastrami sandwiches for dinner and drink and argue into the early hours of the morning. What I had heard was almost true. Allen Ginsberg had a favorite seat until he left, a few years before I arrived. Jack Kerouac had a booth in the back before he took off for somewhere else, a few years before I came down from college. The bar was a long horseshoe, amber bottles rested on shelves beneath the counter. In a corner of the room trays of corned beef and pastrami, stacks of rye bread, waited for orders, beer glasses rested on the tabletops of the booths in the back. The bar smelled of beer and perhaps a little urine from the bathrooms in the rear, and certainly male hormones, a lesser number of female hormones, powders, potions, and sweat. I was wearing a pink sweater with a few holes in it. I was shy and, I thought, conspicuous. In a room alone where no one else seemed to be alone, I stared at the walls, pretending to be engrossed in profound thought. And then there was a slight motion at my side, a frail, small boy with blond hair falling over his forehead was talking to me. He was talking to me about the genius of Ezra Pound. I can't remember if I said what I thought or I didn't. But what I thought was that a genius needed a moral light and without that light whatever he wrote was useless. I would not forgive Ezra Pound that night and not on any night that followed. The boy who was talking to me was a poet. "That man over there," he said to me, "I make a pass at him every night and he brushes me away. He knows my name but he won't say it." Which is how I met Donald and realized that my first friend in the bar was not interested in girls, at least not for illicit purposes, not for the purposes that would render me an unfit wife for the sons of my mother's friends. Nevertheless Donald and I drank together and he promised me a copy of H.D.'s poems, a friend of Pound's, a woman who loved women. All this was very interesting and I drove back to Sarah Lawrence on the Bronx River Parkway, stars above, hair blowing wild in the wind, pleased. I would go back. I did go back.

I was reading *Crime and Punishment* in my Russian

literature class. I was reading À *la recherche du temps perdu* in my French class. I was reading about Occam's razor and Hegel in my intellectual history class. I was thinking that the pain of living would drown me one day but not yet. Now I was riveted by the sight of the human calamity. I wanted to know everything. A girl on my dormitory floor tried to kill herself and ended up in the hospital. A friend of mine had an abortion in Pennsylvania and then developed a raging fever and was finally convinced to go to the infirmary. In the local hospital she lost her womb but saved her life and dropped out of school. So many important matters were simply whispered behind locked doors. It was said, maybe it was all rumor, that my favorite professor was having an affair with a classmate. He already had a Sarah Lawrence wife and had divorced an earlier one. My history professor was having an affair with the girl who lived across the hall. She had deep sad brown eyes and seemed like one of Peter Pan's whimsical boys, very lost. Another of my professors who had written a famous book was having an affair with a student who played the violin. There was talk that the president of the college was too fond of a male member of the Art Department. All this was in the fifties when the lid was on. Under the lid there was fusion and fission and splitting of emotions into an explosion waiting to happen.

So at night I left the campus that sat up the road from the well-groomed houses and the main street of a small town populated by bankers and lawyers and their wives and children. I went to the West End Bar, driving down the parkway into the city, looking at the reaching branches of the single tree that stood at the top of the hill right after the tollbooth, looking out on the Hudson River, looking down on the George Washington Bridge. The tree, a not-so-robust maple, had survived the building of the road, did all the normal seasonal things that trees should do. I took it as my totem. I nodded to it each time I passed.

I didn't drink in the bar. I ordered a whiskey sour and ate the cherry. I always wore blue jeans. In those years proper girls wore skirts with cinched waists. They did not wear pants of any kind, except those of us who early, before the fashion turned, wanted to look like we made something with our hands, we belonged to the country of artists whose passport seemed to be blue jeans and a black T-shirt and sandals. I painted my eyes with black-inked brushes but wore no lipstick. This uniform showed everyone I was interested in sin, the kind someone could write about. What I was after was words. Perhaps money would have been a better bet.

I considered Prince Hal drinking in the tavern with Falstaff. Was I Prince Hal pretending to be one of the fellows when at any moment I could go back to my palace on Park Avenue, put on a pretty dress, and change my life? Was I a fraud? The answer is yes, yes I could have changed my mind like Prince Hal, but no, I meant it. I thought I was free of my past, my place, and airborne as a mayfly. I was exhilarated and terrified. Isn't that what it means to be an American? I was not a Jewish girl, not a New Yorker who had gone to a private girls' school, not the granddaughter of a man who founded a shirt company from the back of his pushcart. I was free to follow Paul Bowles to Morocco, to find Henry Miller in the hills of California, to visit the grave of Balzac, or to travel with Ernest to Kilimanjaro and stand in the brush while the rhinoceros charged past. I would have followed Hans Castorp into battle if I had been able. I would have held his hand as he died and watched in horror as his blood seeped into the ground. I would have nursed Seymour Glass back to health. I did understand that fictional characters, dead authors, and aged writers have limited choices.

1952: I am at a girls' school. We are having a Christmas dance at the Plaza Hotel in the grand ballroom. It is my junior year. This is a dance that even the Jewish girls can attend since it is open to all the students in the class. I have a date who is the son of a friend of my mother's who goes to a boys' prep school and is in town for the holiday. He picks me up at the door and gives me a small orchid which I pin to my dress above my breast. My dress is yellow with pink flowers at the edge. My hair is black and brushed into obedience. My date is shy but that's all right, I can put him at ease. There is a band playing, a Lester Lanin–style band, there are chaperones who stand discreetly behind pillars paying little attention. There are Christmas decorations on all the tables and the lights blink with promise. Out of the corner of my eye I see a tall boy, thin as a rail, with long graceful hands, and he is dancing like a gazelle, his arms around a girl dip her forward and back. His feet fly across the floor. His face is long and there is something I see, even in the quick glance, dark in his eyes, as if he doesn't belong with the others.

And then I see him sitting at a table with another boy and I stop dancing for a moment and explain to my date that the flower pin is hurting me and I take my orchid and I place it on the table in front of the tall stranger and I look him in the face and say nothing. I return to the dance floor and soon he cuts in and my date moves to the side and I am dancing with the boy with long legs and long arms and he twirls me around and then the band plays the Charleston and he and I do the Charleston and everyone gathers around to watch us. I am a good dancer but he is a great dancer. It turns out he has been taking ballet lessons. And then we do the Lindy Hop and then we samba and soon we leave the dance floor and he is smoking outside on the steps of the Plaza.

HE IS A scholarship student from an outer borough. He has failed the SATs because he arrived at the testing place too drunk to sit in his chair. He is a poet. He says that only poetry can save mankind from hell. He bends over me. He tells me his mother has died but that she told him he must marry a rich girl. I am a rich girl. I want him to marry me.

Outside of the men's room, behind a potted plant with Christmas bulbs wrapped around it, we kiss and kiss and I am as happy as I have ever been. The bones of my corset are piercing my chest. I worry that the chaperones will see us. I worry that my date is looking for me. I worry that I will never learn to inhale a cigarette without coughing. I think of *Forever Amber*. Dresses ripped with passion. I don't think of madness. I think of dancing on tables, of watching the moon sink over the Mediterranean Sea and I think of genius, the wonder of it, the daring of it, the anti–golf course of it, the anti–financial sheet of it, the anti–day after day of it, the pleasure of crashing a small plane into the rough Atlantic seas. I think I am blessed by Jack's clear eyes, not warm eyes, not loving eyes, but eyes that see in the dark, devil's eyes. Lucky me. The kissing is fine but the conquest is better. He pulls out a small thermos of scotch and offers me some. It tastes terrible. I pretend to like it. I go off to find my date, my boring date. My life is determined.

1962: I am a single woman again. At George Plimpton's one Friday night I sat down on the lap of a sculptor who made abstract shapes out of iron scraps. He was just getting a reputation and he wore overalls and a work shirt and he had a dark beard and his eyes were red-rimmed from some sin or other or perhaps just lack of sleep. He stroked the back of my neck with his strong hand and led me into the hallway. He came home with me and although he did not speak very much, his body was sufficiently eloquent. He played with the child over her breakfast and told her that one day she would come and see his big dog. When he left I felt joy. In my mind I moved out of the apartment my mother had bought for my ex-husband and me and moved with him to a loft in Queens and in my mind I saw us sleeping together on a mattress in a cabin in the woods he told me that he owned high in the Catskills. I took the child to school. I sat down to a second cup of coffee and the phone rang. It was his wife. He hadn't told me about his wife. She said she thought I should know she wasn't stable and prone to set fires. The next week when I saw him at the Plimpton party I looked right through him. He turned away from me. If I was going to the dark forest with a sculptor it would have to be another.

1951: There was a boy I met at a dance. His name was Roger. We did the Lindy together. He was earnest. He didn't need me to ask him what his favorite sport was. He talked about his hope for racial equality in this country. He told me to read Howard Fast. I gave him my phone number. I told my mother the dance had been boring but it hadn't been. He invited me to go with him to a Pete Seeger concert down in the Village. I wore a corset, stiff and harsh; it pinched my waist. I wore a petticoat under my skirt. I still bit my fingernails down to the cuticle. He had thick glasses and a mop of unruly hair. He came to pick me up and said hello to the maid who opened the door. He asked her name and shook her hand. She was astounded. So was I. We rode the bus downtown. By the time we arrived at the church basement where the concert was about to begin I was wishing with all my heart that I could go to Spain and fight the Falangists as Roger's father had done. I imagined myself as a nurse rushing forward to treat the wounded. And then there was Pete Seeger. He was a friend of Roger's family and so I was introduced to him before the concert. If Pete Seeger were the pied piper I would have followed him right into the cave. "Turn, turn, turn . . . A time to be born, a time to die," "It aint quite this simple, so I better explain, Just why you got to ride on the union train." This last line particularly thrilled me, the granddaughter of a man who had founded a shirt company. I was drawn into

the rocking of the audience as we joined in the chorus: it was
the holding hands with strangers, it was the thought that it didn't
have to be the way it was, it was the thrill of betrayal. I had been
born in the enemy camp. And now I had crossed over. It wasn't
simply exciting. It was sublime. A new sensation came over me,
tingling up my spine. Perhaps it was love.

My father hated Communists, pinkos and Reds, Commie
bastards, he said, Commie jerks, he said, Commies belonged in
jail, all of them, he said. Commies should all get the chair like
the Rosenbergs, he said. I began to buy the *Daily Worker* at the
corner newsstand. I would read it and throw it away before I
went home. My father said Commies deserved to be branded on
their foreheads or their asses. My father believed that we should
drop the bomb on Moscow before they dropped it on us. This
made Roger even more appealing than he might otherwise have
been. Justice for the poor, the Negro, the working man, seemed
to me, a girl from Park Avenue, righteous. I had not heard about
the gulags or the purges or the famines. Neither had Roger or he
forgot to mention them to me.

I kissed Roger in the hall outside my apartment. Long after
Roger disappeared from my life I still read the *Daily Worker*. I
hoped that justice was possible in an obviously unjust and
dangerous world.

1961: We are having a movie screening at our apartment.
I am not yet divorced but I am beginning to feel unmoored,
blurred. The movie was made by two brothers. They are avant-

garde filmmakers who work with handheld cameras. They are
the anti-Hollywood, the pre–Andy Warhol filmmakers, the
downtown art center of rebellion and resistance to Hollywood.
We have invited a few people over. The child is asleep in the
bedroom. One of the brothers is a thin scraggly man, perhaps
with a little beard though I am not sure. He has strange eyes. He
seems like a starving bird hopping around from chair to chair.
Into the room comes Salvador Dalí, invited by the filmmakers.
He is accompanied by his very much younger girlfriend who has
just graduated from the convent school where her movie-star
mother had placed her. She has come to New York to study
acting. She is wispy and yet magnificent, her beauty is so pure,
her smile so sweet, her hands white and clasped together shyly.
Her name is Mia Farrow. Salvador Dalí explains that he has just
made a film with her in which he had his naked self covered in
whipped cream and then turned the camera on while Mia
licked him clean. I didn't say a word but I looked at the older
portly Dalí and imagined it all. I didn't want to react as if I were
a nun but I did feel my stomach flip. Mia sat on the other side of
the room. Was she eighteen or seventeen? I knew about
absurdity, about surrealism, about épater le bourgeoisie, and still
I was not clear. Was this art or was it not?

    I don't remember the films the brothers showed or why they
were showing them in our apartment. Perhaps they were raising
money but from whom I can't imagine. Peter Matthiessen was
there with his second wife. I tried not to feel jealous of her but I
was. Peter Matthiessen was not just a long-legged prep school–
looking man; he also had appeared to be a man who hunted and

climbed mountains and spoke in native languages and lay down in the tall grass and let bugs crawl over his chest. He had a quiet fierce intelligence that came from his eyes, the cut of his jaw. I had no evidence for my sudden affection. I thought that he cared, that he could love someone, that a wise goodness was moving within him, not like his friends, not like Jack, not like George, not like me. Of course I had no evidence for that. It may have been a romantic illusion. He might have just robbed a bank. But I knew in the marrow of my bones that I would have been devoted to him if I had met him in time, in Paris when *The Paris Review* was founded, before he met his first wife, Patsy, who seemed to me when I met her later so protected by birth, by grace, I could hardly believe the stories I heard that chaos had dragged her too into the back alleys. I had no glamour, no shine like hers. But I would have been devoted. All that I thought as the film flickered, dark moody shadows, no plot to be unfolded, on the screen we had set up at the front of the room.

1959: One night when Jack was out an encyclopedia salesman came to the door. The set was expensive but could be paid for in installments at $25 a month. I wanted the encyclopedia. It contained all the facts about the known world, the depths of oceans, the locations of mountains, the names of rare animals, the populations of distant lands. I wanted to know all the facts. I thought that if I had the encyclopedia I could become a learned person, sated with the truth of things. It wasn't the salesman. It was my lust for the encyclopedia from A to Z. It arrived a week later. I placed the volumes on a bookshelf and the look of them, the leather bindings, the gold lettering reassured me. But then at the end of the month when the coupons came and payment was due, I didn't have the $25 in my bank account. My husband had taken the balance and turned it into golden liquid and poured it down his throat. I would send $15 and a pleading note. Sometimes I ignored the coupon and soon received a threatening letter about repossession of my books. I wanted to keep them. But I could see that I had made a bad mistake. I skipped lunch. I let my shoes become scuffed and out of shape. I borrowed from my mother again and again. The books on the shelf became a burden. I wanted to return them. I wished they would take them away. But they never did. I dreaded the envelope with the payment request. Month after month it came. Once I told my mother I had to pay a dentist. Once I told her I needed a haircut. At last the company gave up on me. They stopped sending dunning letters. No one came to the door to reclaim the encyclopedia. I didn't open its pages. I had stolen it and was ashamed. I had almost paid it all but not quite.

I NEEDED THE JOB so I kept on working. My husband finished the play. It was about Orestes. It was about sexual sin. It was about political power. When I typed the last lines I thought I was probably the most fortunate woman in the world. I went to my parents' friends and raised $250 from each couple and some from my mother and found a producer willing to do the play if I brought in the money. The play opened in a very small theater above the Ukrainian meeting hall in the East Village. The night it opened Jack and I and the set designer left the after-play celebration and walked through the streets of the real Broadway, the one with the big lights, and we linked arms and shouted at the theaters, "We're here. We are coming, get out of the way." I could taste the fame that was approaching. I could breathe the air of the important folks that had dinner at Sardi's and ate cheesecake at Lindy's. I thought that now that success had come Jack would become sane and put his hand in mine forevermore.

I thought I should have a reward for my part in this success. I got pregnant.

1964: I think I need to find a father for the child. I know that a home with two parents is better for the security of the child. My friend Fran from the playground whose husband is a neurosurgeon at a large hospital introduces me to another friend who is also the wife of a doctor. She invites me to a dinner party. I will start to know doctors, I think. I dress carefully. I sit at the table, the only single person there, and join in the conversation. I am having a good time but as soon as the dessert plates are removed the men all move off to the far corner of the room and the women gather around the couch. I join the women. They talk about brands of diapers. They talk about preschool teachers and they talk about the hours their children nap or sleep. They talk about the clever things their children have said. They talk about babysitting problems. Across the room I hear something about a terrible accident in the operating room. I want to hear the end of the story but I can't betray my sex and move across the floor. I hear the men talking about President Kennedy and someone is doubting that he wrote his own speeches. I had an opinion on that but I couldn't move. I go home and decide that I will not become a doctor's wife after all.

1963: A few months after Doc Humes visited me in the Berkshires he and his family went off to England to live and work. I never saw him again. I heard reports. He had dropped acid with a theater critic named Kenneth Tynan. He had not come out of the trip. He had been hospitalized. His wife had another baby, their fourth girl. I knew it would be hard, so many children and Doc, Doc in the hospital. But I envied her. I wanted more children. I wanted to be a mother of many. My love for my child saved me from the rising tides of sorrow. If I had more children my levee would be higher, stronger. I understood why Doc's wife had given birth to another child. This was her power. This was her purpose. This was her trial. This was her work. Mine too. I had to live. I had to be strong. I had to take care of my child. The Child Development Center said she needed a powerful tranquilizer. It would affect her growth. It might leave her with permanent tremors. It had never been given to children before. I declined. I did take her once a week to a therapist who played with her. She still wept if I left the house.

Later I heard a rumor that Doc had come out of the hospital.

He was a danger to his wife and children. I heard they were returning to the United States without him. I heard that he was no longer sane, not even sometimes. He would write no more best sellers. He would have no more inventive ideas. He would not found another literary magazine like *The Paris Review*. He would spend the rest of his life thinking about the FBI and the way they were pursuing him and he had one theory after another about alien forces controlling our destiny. Maybe he was right—after all the difference between a prophet and a madman is a matter of opinion.

1956: I am on a summer trip. Our group from Sarah Lawrence was going to study French in a small school for foreign students. It was on the Left Bank. I wanted to be on the Left Bank. It is late June when we sail. The boat rocks across the sea and I stand at the rail throwing wishes out onto the receding foam. Paris is where Jake Barnes loved despite some mysterious damage to his parts that I couldn't quite imagine but nevertheless interested me enormously. Paris is where Josephine Baker sang into the dawn and Sara and Gerald Murphy brought their sons who would later die and where James Baldwin drank Pernod at Les Deux Magots on the Left Bank and wrote in his notebook. Paris is where the Baron de Charlus walked down dark alleys to unmarked doors behind which waited the flesh he would mark in some way that also was not quite clear to me although I read the passages several times through. Paris is where Swann dreamed of Odette and André Gide lost his faith and where his wife burned his letters because he went to Egypt and fell in love with a boy. Paris is where Jewish children were rounded up and waited days in the railway station for the trains that would carry them to their deaths.

I find a café. I order in French. I am wearing my favorite sweater. It has a few holes in it. I am wearing blue jeans and dark eye makeup. I am the anti-Smith girl. Everything about me announces that I am opposed to country clubs everywhere. I am the enemy of suburban lawns and gold bracelets, fraternities, Fascists, and stockbrokers, and all that interests me is the making of art, the writing of poetry, the life of rebellion. I think I am a nonconformist but as I look about me in the bar at the other girls I see that I am wearing a uniform. All the other women look like me, pale, free of nail polish, wearing black leotards and thick sandals, a toughness in their straight backs, ink stains on the fingers, notebooks in the lap, and a nervous blinking of the eye.

At Sarah Lawrence I had taken a course in writing with a poet named Horace Gregory. He did not believe that the personal was a subject fit for public consumption. He did not believe that the thoughts of women were worth the paper they were written on. He said so, often. He said so to a girl who had spent six weeks in a motel in Reno, Nevada, getting a divorce and written about her experiences in the motel bar. Bitter and sad her words were. She wrote like an avenging angel. I was awed. Horace Gregory was not. He said to her, "What makes you think anyone cares about your divorce?" I had cared. But I had no heroic subject to offer. I had no encounters with raging bulls. I had not and would not be going to war. I knew nothing about sex or death. I had nothing to say. I had no story. I became a muse instead of a writer. The costume fit.

This sudden and overwhelming desire to bring coffee to the side of a writer, to wash his socks, to stare down his enemies, internal or external, seems inexplicable in the light of the following turns of history. But at the time it was adaptive, the way the leopard got his spots and the snake his nasty rattle. That statement is both true and untrue because I had other, more personal reasons to abandon my notebooks in a trash can on the Upper West Side. I lacked courage. I was not as much a warrior as a housewife in waiting, another girl who would love the wrong man for reasons that must have sounded bizarre even to the therapist who heard them years later.

I wanted to study life. I preferred tragedy to comedy. I was hoping that by the end of the summer I would understand the Rilke poems I had slipped into my suitcase along with the silk nightgown my mother had purchased at Bergdorf Goodman for my trip.

Everything about Paris caused me to fill with grand emotion. Perhaps it was lust, not in the pornographic sense but in the desire to know, to see, to feel, to become a part of the arches and the trees in the park and the smoke in the cafés and the dead rabbits hanging in the window of the butchers and to cross the wide streets and to know that something momentous was going to happen to me soon. I ached from the desire to shed my skin and become . . . what? I smoked Gauloises after Gauloises, grasping the blue package as if it were my ticket to immortality. I drank coffee, black as the eyeliner I wore. I went out alone. I didn't want to be seen with my American classmates. Destiny would not find me if I were hiding in a group. I went to the Louvre and stared at the *Mona Lisa*. Mostly I saw my own face in the reflection of the glass. I hoped I was moved by the painting's extraordinary beauty but perhaps not. Also much to my distress I discovered I couldn't inhale my cigarette because it made me cough, a spasm grabbed my chest and brought tears to my eyes which made my eye makeup run so I learned how to puff very gently, blow out very quickly, a deceptive move that still allowed me the pleasure of lighting up and leaning away from the wind and watching the small glow at the tip increase its heat, burn away. I sat in the chair that Richard Wright had sat in, a notebook on the table before him, writing *Native Son*. Or so the waiter told me.

So goodbye to my childhood of tennis lessons and scary stories around the campfire. Goodbye to parents, uncles, and aunts who had not read George Eliot or James Joyce. Goodbye to corsets and stockings and mad money stuffed in little pocketbooks decorated with rhinestones. Goodbye to all those who didn't know that the wrong side had won the Spanish civil war. And all those goodbyes made me sad. I walked the streets haunted by my own visions of past and future. But at least I walked and walked. From time to time I would find an empty table at a promising café, order a *sandwich jambon*, a lemonade, and place myself in harm's way, seeking harm the way a salmon seeks its breeding ground. I hoped to meet a writer and fix him dinner eternally.

AND THEN one morning, the ash from my Gauloises spilling into my saucer, I glanced up and saw a young man with a copy of Rilke poems, the same small yellow book I owned, in his hand at the next table. He was reading. He hadn't noticed me. I rattled my cup. I dropped my purse loudly on the ground. I shook the table until it squeaked and he looked up and saw me. I tried to look uninterested. He was interested. He stood up. I thought perhaps he was calling for the waiter to pay his check and off he would go but he came over to my table. "*Bonjour,*" he said and I knew he was American. Mark Sullivan from Brooklyn, graduate of Stuyvesant High School and City College, recipient of a Fulbright to Finland where he had spent the year in the cold endless night of the north. He was traveling for the summer with the money he had saved. He was a writer, a not-yet-published writer. He had dark eyes and the beginnings of a beard around his chin. He read me a Rilke poem. We took a long walk and I gave him my hand. I forgot about my French class. I forgot about modesty and caution. In the Tuileries he reached into a small fenced-in garden and pulled out a white daisy and put it in my hair. If you had told me at that moment that my mother still existed and was playing canasta by the pool at her country club I would not have believed you. I had cleaned the surface of my mind with such thoroughness that only the present remained and the future promised.

He had rented a room on the top floor of a small house on a winding street. His attic window looked out on the peaked roof across the street, at the old pipes and bent tanks that stretched out as far as the eye could see. There was no snow. It was summer. So the scene was not a Utrillo. Perhaps there were flower pots with red geraniums in the window on the other side of the street, perhaps there was a musician practicing his piano on the floor below. No one was coughing from tuberculosis in the room next door. As I slipped off my dress and stood there in my pink slip, I rose like a balloon whose owner releases the string.

The bedspread smelled of bleach. Through the windows came the sounds of horns, of cars turning down the street. Out of the corner of my eye I saw a church steeple or at least the base of it and a row of black birds on a stone ledge. Terror clamped me closed and no amount of eager pressure could open the gate. He was sweating. I was crying. Was I a freak of nature or was I simply hearing my mother's voice, no man will have you if another has had you? Was I thinking of conception, not so immaculate, ending in blood and infection and fever and death? Was I thinking of girls picked up by serial killers who placed their hands about the throat and broke necks in their fury? All I know for certain is that it was impossible. I was a flower that could not be deflowered. It is hard to understand that now when twelve-year-olds in kneesocks are playing games after school that I didn't know existed until I read Henry Miller and was still confused as to how and what exactly was happening on the page before me. I was intent on freedom from the rules. I had rebellion clearly in mind but the mind did not know itself and the body wet with effort had to admit defeat.

What we did next: go to a hospital. I thought perhaps I had cancer. I thought perhaps I was born with a deformity. On the taxi ride to the American hospital Mark held my hand and stroked my thigh. He was worried too. He didn't believe in too clean a shave. He carried his rucksack with his notebook in it. I knew he was thinking this is an experience I can write about. In the taxi there was a heavy space between us where his words floated and his thoughts collided with the anxiety that rushed out of my body and covered my shame at this failure with a false calm, a false quiet.

The doctor in the emergency room spoke English with a charming French accent. He was perfectly unflustered as if I had presented with a sprained ankle. What was sprained of course was far more intimate and humiliating than an ankle. Covered with a white sheet, draped in a hospital gown I lay back on the examining table and considered the possibility that I might never have children, never know the world as a woman should, never experience the world that I had read about, never understand what Anaïs Nin was talking about. Like a blind person or a nun I would spend the rest of my life confined to the limits of my own body. I felt some pain, some poking as the doctor under the sheet examined me. He delivered the verdict. I was fine. He told me to go home, take a hot bath, and have a glass of wine. "Nothing is wrong," he said, "you are just without experience." This itself was an experience. Let me forget this immediately, I said to myself. Repress it, deny it, obliterate it from my memory. I have forgotten the name of the street we were on. I have forgotten the color of the bedsheets. I have forgotten the names of the girls who were on the trip to Paris with me. But the rest remains just as it was, unchanged by time.

We went back to the room, up the stairs, looked out over the rooftops of Paris, saw the cars below rush down the narrow street, and we had a glass of wine. There was no bathtub. I lay down on the bed and we tried again. I was sweating. I could smell myself. I was embarrassed by the smell. But this time he entered. There was some pain but not so much. There was a spot of blood. I lay on the bed and fell asleep to the sound of his typewriter's tap tap tap, the snap of the return lever, the sound of paper inserted and withdrawn. This was the sound of creation, defiance, a world that would be set afire with words, his words. I would never be a girl who played golf. I would never be a woman whose life sped by in a flip of aces, kings, and queens flashing across the card table. If there was a God who would punish me for my sins, and I doubted it, I would move too fast for Him to find me. If all was meaningless then I would pledge myself to the Ancient Mariner who had a way with words. Now I would follow the bulls wherever the bulls were running.

Mark wore a dirty gray T-shirt. He wore blue jeans and sandals and he was always half shaved. He sketched, with charcoal, a drawing of himself that he gave to me. I placed it in my suitcase between my copy of Thomas Mann's *The Magic Mountain* and Jean-Paul Sartre's *No Exit*. And off I went without a word to the school where I was enrolled, to the girls I had arrived with weeks before. We were going to Spain, on the remains of Mark's Fulbright and on the traveler's checks I kept in my underwear.

It may not be possible to explain how beautiful a railroad station appears to a girl who is no longer a virgin. The whistles, the lacework black steel overhead, the sounds of wheel on track, the smell of orange and whiskey, garlic and human sweat, the baskets and boxes, and flowers and babies, the loaves of bread, the bare backs of women, the caps of men, the rolling of luggage carts, the waving of passengers to those on the platform, seemed like a personal invitation and Mark would carry me there — wherever there was. Even then I knew I was not headed toward Paradise. I wanted no part of Paradise. And in the train station, it came to me again, the children herded into cattle cars and headed for Auschwitz. It came to me that trains were the wagons that brought the innocents to slaughter. This hadn't occurred to Mark. It wasn't his vocabulary. It was mine, and even as I climbed the steps to our car I remembered to feel fear, no not fear, an echo of fear, a tremor of mistrust, that rippled through the journey at each clamor of bells signaling the bars at the crossing going down, rising up. Through the Pyrenees the hunted Jews had climbed to safety. At least some of them. I looked out the window at the fields and the hills and the cows who had ignored the strangers hauling their small suitcases upward in haste. At the station stops we jumped out onto the platform and purchased oranges, strawberries, water from the vendors who called to us. The sun passed over the fields, the towns, the churches, the cities, the villages and when it was dark I put my head against Mark's shoulder and slept.

It is true what they said about the fifties. You really were supposed to behave. You wanted to look like all those around you and to keep your lawn free of floating leaves and nasty weeds. You wanted to live inside the lines where the ordinariness of everything would protect you from the dragons that lay at the edge of the map ready to blow fire in your face if you strayed off course, to the edge of the known world. Underneath the shirts and ties, underneath the crinolines and corsets, the hearts of men and women beat with all the old familiar regrets, the same encounters with mortality that had brought the previous generations to their knees in prayer. The lines of what was allowed and what was not were broad, clear, and not up for discussion. Which isn't to say that a lot of people didn't get pregnant when they ought not, and a lot of people didn't fall down drunk when uprightness was the code of the day and a lot of people smothered disappointments in mounds of Jell-O topped with a dollop of whipped cream. But disorder, sexual pleasure was kept behind the fence, your fence, your neighbor's fence, the apartment door. Don't ever let a boy see menstrual blood. Don't ever let him get to second base. Don't ever admit you need money, love, a lawyer. Don't ever be seen carrying a bottle of liquor. Put it in a paper bag. Don't ever wear clothes that make you look different. Never go out of the house without your face on. And all of this was to keep life at bay, life like the big waves at the shore, to be rushed into, to be ridden up and down, life that tasted of salt and could pull you out over your head, that kind of life was to be avoided at all costs and that was just the life I was seeking.

The social rules wanted me, just the way Uncle Sam wanted the boys my age to go to Korea.

We were in Barcelona. We took a room in a tenement just off the wharf where the prostitutes sat in the open bars and beckoned to passersby. We were on the top floor with a small balcony that overlooked a cobblestone courtyard. There was laundry on lines stretched from one side to the other and below us peddlers called to the housewives, selling fresh fish, shrimp, octopus, bread. At evening time a man came into the courtyard with a large basket in his arms. He called up into the air but he had no words only terrible sounds, guttural sounds that came from his throat. He was selling rope for hanging the wash from terrace to terrace. The bartender at the corner café told me that the man's tongue had been pulled out by the Fascists during the war. The war was long over but tongues do not grow back.

We went to cathedrals and museums like ordinary tourists. We sat in grand parks and we looked out at the salt-smelling sea. I ate little bits of eel and octopus and squid floating in olive oil, but the thing I remember best is the sound coming from the throat of the man without a tongue, rising up in the courtyard, a monument to civilization or its discontents.

Here was Europe, the stones were worn with years, the corners narrow and the streets pulsed like veins in an ancient body, swollen, ugly, shaped by stories, war stories, sickness stories, demons, real and unreal. I understood—America was clean, deodorized, and shallow, empty of heart, scrubbed of memory, devoid of passion, missing great sorrows, cathedral bells that fairly moaned and cornices sporting suffering saints. Once

Jews had practiced medicine and law and commerce here. But
then the king and queen at the bidding of the church forced
them to leave. The representatives of the crown desiccated
synagogues and places where the Torah had rested behind
embroidered curtains. Marrano Jews, in the dark with the
curtains drawn, lit candles and whispered their prayers hastily.
Sometimes they were caught and tortured in iron maidens, in
contraptions of steel, on beds of nails. Sometimes they starved to
death in dungeons. I saw a hard emptiness in the Madonna's
eyes, in the emaciated limbs of Christ suffering on his cross. The
candles glowed against the stone walls and the tapestries of
angels and wise men hung on the walls like ancient moss against
a tree but the victory was mine. I was alive.

Everything smelled in the street, urine, wine, sweat, animal
waste, and in the rank odor I learned the fact of decay,
something I had not noticed in America.

Mark sits on a wooden chair, his typewriter on his lap. He
is in his undershirt on the balcony and I am naked on the bed.
I pose my body like the Manet nude. I pose my body like a
Goya. I think of my freedom as a gift. I decide I want to go to a
whorehouse. I want to see whores where they work. Something
I want to understand and I don't. That night I dress as a boy. I
wear Mark's shirt. I wear a cap over my hair. I practice standing
and walking like a boy. I follow Mark, who finds a brothel. We
enter together. I stand with a large group of men in a hall while
girls in high heels and with little strings over their genitals walk
back and forth on a platform at one end of the room. When a
man wants a particular girl he signals to a midget sitting on a

corner of the platform and then the man and the girl disappear
into the back of the house. All I can see is an orange light
blinking in the distance, casting a shadow on a curtain. It is hot
and noisy. Smoke is everywhere. Ashes fall to the ground,
cigarette butts pile up on the floor. There is laughter, nervous
laughter, dirty laughter, grunts, lewd sucking sounds. It is hot,
we are pressed together, shoulder to shoulder. I have trouble
seeing the platform. I stand on tiptoe. A wisp of hair falls out of
my cap. I do not speak Spanish but I understand when a tall
policeman pulls at my arm and gestures to me to follow him.
Mark comes with me. Outside the policeman speaks in loud
and angry Spanish. I explain I only speak English. A passerby
stops to interpret. It seems that the church allows the brothels to
operate as they will, but children under seventeen are not
allowed and the policeman thought I was an underage boy, not
yet shaving, and was preparing to arrest me. I explained that I
was an American girl, just a curious girl, not intending to break
a law. I spent the night in a Spanish jail, on a hard bench. In the
morning someone Mark had contacted from the American
embassy came and arranged for my release. The man from the
embassy was disgusted with me. We are contacting your
parents, he said. My parents thought I was in Paris. It didn't
matter. They couldn't reach me across the sea and what could
they say after all.

I would never forget the odor of lust and sweat and beer and
perfume and bleach in the hall of that brothel. It made me long
for the sea.

We walked through Barcelona, Mark's arm around my

shoulder or his hand in mine. We went through a narrow street. There were cobblestones on the ground, the smell of fish in the air, then out from under the arches of a gray building with wide windowsills and decorative columns, an old building, cracks in the plaster everywhere, came a sudden sound like wind released from a balloon and then a thousand screeches, a screaming without tone or meaning. A colony of bats was flying just above our heads. Mark's hand in mine tightened. His face turned red and sweat was pouring through his shirt. His legs were shaking. He was afraid of the bats. I didn't want them in my hair but they seemed to have no interest in my hair so I was calm. I reassured Mark. They are not attacking us. He couldn't talk. He dropped to his knees and put his head in his hands. I could see tears dropping on the stones. He shut his eyes tight. He would not open them. He would not move forward or back. The sound above us stopped. Still he would not open his eyes. I promised that the bats were gone. I helped Mark stand. He kept his eyes closed and I led him, as if he were a blind man, unused to his blindness, afraid of every step, down the long curving uphill street till we came to a crossing that led to a wide avenue. At last he opened his eyes. It was the first time in my life that another person needed me, so literally, so immediately. In gratitude I leaned against his warm and wet body. What came then was, if not love, at least an emotion that was unfamiliar, and welcome.

Later we sat in a small bar, drinking beer. Mark told me when he was six years old he had been bitten by a squirrel in Central Park. He had been trying to feed the squirrel a peanut that he held out in the palm of his hand and the animal's tail was long and looked soft to the touch and so he reached for it and held it tightly and the squirrel bit him on his finger and scratched at his hands. Afterward he had endured days and days of terrible shots, needles in his stomach to prevent rabies. I understood. He had every right to be afraid of bats. I thought of him, a little boy, lying on the steel table in the doctor's office, his shirt pulled up, his pants loosened, his child's belt resting on the top of his thighs, and the needle coming closer and closer.

I kissed Mark's barely shaved chin. I wished I could explain to him what had bitten me, but my story was so long and no longer had anything to do with my real self, the self that was drinking beer by the Mediterranean, sitting on a high stool next to a man who had taken out his notebook and was writing in his large looping hand. Perhaps he was writing about me.

Perhaps he was not. I was bored. I went for a walk and bought an ice and when I returned to the bar Mark was on his third beer and he was still writing.

Because of the bats Mark wanted to leave Barcelona and go to an island off the coast of France. We went by a small ferry (or was it a large motorboat?). The island we were going to was Île du Levant. It was a nudist island. As the boat docked we removed all our clothes and stuffed them in our luggage. Naked except for the sandals on my feet I disembarked and walked past the dozen or so people, men and women and children, all naked, waiting for the arrival of the ferry. I wanted to put my arms across my chest. I wanted a fig leaf. I wanted my skirt back.

But it was clear in this place everyone was nude and no one broke the code—the code of normalcy, although I saw nothing normal about male genitals hanging down as naturally as bananas on a tree. I could tell you weren't supposed to stare or stop moving forward on the path, or behave in any way that would make a fellow guest on the island feel observed. On the other hand, observing was surely the point.

I soon found out that there were priests who vacationed here. There were young lovers and old married couples who came to cure malaria caught on business stays in India, there were families who believed that the human body without clothes was a sacred object. There were naked boys selling beads. You were allowed to wear beads and the colorful glass strung around everyone's neck somehow lent spice to the bodies that passed by. Plain nakedness was too plain. It soon bored. There was in the midst of this sun and salt and smell of coconut oils and tanning butters a swarm of cameras. It seemed that almost every other male on the island had a camera on his blanket or worn about his neck. The custom was that the man with the camera would approach the husband, father, boyfriend of some woman, would ask permission to take her photograph. These photos, it was explained to me, would be exchanged between the men all through the cold winter months. Why, I asked. No one explained. I could hardly sit down on my blanket and daydream about the rest of my life because I was constantly asked to stand, here or there, on this rock or that, with my back to the sun or my arms around a tree trunk, or with a flower in my hand. Mark gave permission to everyone who asked to take my picture. All the women were being photographed. It seemed churlish to protest, and after all why would I not give pleasure to a man at his desk in February, what was I hiding, or withholding? I let everyone photograph me. I practiced my French. I made a friend of a Spanish student who had tuberculosis and needed to be in the sun. I met a priest who loved to talk to American girls about his hero: Frank Sinatra. Naked I spent two weeks, naked I lay with Mark in our small cabin and listened to the sea hit the rocks below. Naked as Eve I became restless.

And then by the light of our flickering kerosene lamp I read the story Mark had been writing in his notebook. It was long. It was serious. It was about death and its inevitability. It was about a forest invaded by a plant disease. A faun spoke aloud. It was awful. Perhaps it wasn't awful. Perhaps I had read too many French writers who could make sentences like blades that grew sharper with each cut. Perhaps I had in mind the heavy tread of Thomas Mann across our emotions. But I thought it was awful. And as I put down the final page and told Mark what a fine piece it was, my heart separated from his and went its own perilous way.

What kind of girl needs a certain kind of sentence to maintain her love for a handsome man who has taken her across the Pyrenees and down to the south of France and bathed nude, eaten nude, slept nude beside her in unexpected and welcomed gentleness? Perhaps I was a gold digger and my gold was literary fame. Perhaps I was simply too much in love with other men, J. D. Salinger for one. Marcel Proust for two. Ernest and F. Scott for three and four. Perhaps I did not want to make love by the pale blue Mediterranean Sea and run the white sand down my legs and let it sift through my fingers like flour for a cake. Perhaps all I wanted was to read. I only wanted a fine writer. I was uninterested in boys with dull manuscripts, boys who would soon see that they had best become merchants or doctors or open a restaurant. I wanted a writer of prose that stunned in its truth, had the power to change a person's landscape. I wanted, in a phrase not yet invented, nothing but shock and awe, printed and bound.

When it was time to take my plane back to America I was there at the airport, browned and sun-kissed in places the girls in my group did not imagine. I embraced Mark at the gate. I ran my fingers over his lips. I touched his eyelids so I could remember how they felt and I hoped never to see him again and I didn't. I showed the self-portrait he had drawn for me to my roommate at college. I taped it on the wall above the typewriter that rested on my wobbly desk. I liked particularly the dark eyes, the few-days-old stubble of a beard, the black curls. I liked the fact that it was a picture pinned to the wall and did not follow me about.

That fall at Sarah Lawrence I found a new love. Albert Camus. I believed it was his diamond prose. I thought it was his cool vision of the world that moved me so deeply. It might also have been the jacket photo. The face was the face of a man who would understand me, me and all his other readers of both sexes as well. I did not expect him to appear in my real world. I just wanted him there on the bookshelf, to look at from time to time, as I considered that the absence of God in my world, the lack of a protecting hand that might stay disaster as it approached, could be filled by a man who wrote with a cool ferocity, who could step into the barren landscape and plant in the hostile soil, words, the right words.

Years later I would read in Philip Roth about his encounter with this woman or that. I would find it strange that he was so interested in the shape of a breast, the length of a thigh, the curve between the humps of the ass. He never read anyone's manuscript as an invitation to foreplay. He was interested in the smell and the juice of his partner. I was interested in the words that could be put on paper afterward. He may have been a misogynist in that his intentions toward women were lustful and sometimes harmful, mostly to himself, but he, at least, was not looking for a writer to make his world whole. He was hoping to find pleasure—he urgently needed to get his penis inside a vagina, which strikes me as far more honest than my preliminary explorations.

1965: I am dating a psychologist who is in training at one of the psychoanalytic institutes. He came to America as a child from Denmark. His father had been a well-known scholar in Copenhagen.

The king was wearing a yellow star. The Jewish community was alerted at synagogue on a Friday night. They went to the shore. Dozens of small fishing boats sailed them to Sweden. The psychologist is ambitious and edgy. He has already divorced a

wife and is looking for another. I am a possibility. I go with him
to a party at the home of a well-known psychologist. We are
sitting on plastic chairs eating from plates on our laps when I
shift in my seat and a searing pain rises through my left calf. I
don't scream but I might have. Quietly I look down and see
blood on the floor below. I catch a glimpse of a retreating black
cat. My black leotard is torn open and blood has stained the
fabric. The scratch is not minor. It is hard for the several
assembled doctors to stop the bleeding. The scratch, the wound,
extends from just below the knee right down to the heel. It will
need stitches. I will need a tetanus shot. "Ah," says the
psychologist who owns the culprit cat, "you must have
frightened him." "I didn't," I say. "Perhaps you stepped on him,"
he says. "No," I say, "I didn't even see him." The psychologist I
am dating does not want to go with me to the emergency room.
He is talking with his colleagues. I go by myself and then go
home with a bandage and elaborate instructions on how to care
for a ripped leg.

I am a cat lover. Still it seems to me that the host might have
put the cat in a closet for the party. It seems to me that my date
might have taken me to the hospital. The next Friday night we
are having a drink on his small terrace sixteen stories above the
street. I lean over the rail to see the cars and the lights of the
restaurant across the way and a desire sweeps over me, a
hurricane-strength urge to throw myself down, to quickly
plunge, headfirst, toward the street. I step back. The child needs
me. The babysitter must be paid. What has come over me? I am

with this man but I am not close to this man although I am glad that he has escaped the Nazis. I am alone which is no reason to go careening down to the street, to end in blood and bones that someone will have to clear away. And what of the child? But it is a reason never to see this man again.

1953: I walked through the living room one spring day with my tennis racket banging against my knee. I wanted my father to get off the phone and drive me to the club where I was to have a lesson. I hear him say, "All right, Judge, we're agreed, $50,000 next week." I wait. "You know what we want, Judge. I know what you want." My father hangs up the phone, picks up his golf clubs. "Were you bribing a judge?" I ask. I try to use the tone you would use to inquire if someone remembered to turn off the lights. My father says, "The other side probably gave him the same amount. I'm making sure the trial will be fair." That seems reasonable and then it doesn't.

Tammany Hall was a part of it all. That is how you became a judge, by being in with the Tammany Hall people. Roy Cohn, who was a cousin of mine—my aunt's nephew—was in with all the big fellows at Tammany Hall. My father said justice was blind and dumb, and he didn't laugh. He never laughed.

I am a good basketball player. My school team needs me. I play the kind of game that sometimes leads me to crash into the gym walls or to fall to the floor headfirst. I spare nothing, forgetting for the time being that there is a law of gravity that applies to me as well as to others. I forget that the game doesn't

matter, that there is nothing to win of worth. I agree to go and
meet the younger brother of David Schine but only after my
basketball practice. That's why I arrive at the '21' Club at the
cocktail hour in my blue gym uniform, with my bloomers
slipping down my thighs, my bobby socks around my ankles,
and my black curly hair unbrushed because my brush had been
forgotten. I carried my school bag, Ovid, algebra, and ancient
history. I walk past the little figures of Negro jockeys in their
colors, hitching posts, souvenirs of the South that was. The
waiter showed me to a table, his face showing no disapproval of
my outfit. He spirited away my camel-hair coat. I would have
gone to the ladies' room but I wasn't sure if I had the money to
give to the women who offered towels to the patrons. And there
was David Schine's brother, hunched over, heavy, round, very
short, acne-covered, not acne like the poppies in the field in *The
Wizard of Oz* but acne real and pus-filled spilling across the
chin, the corners of his mouth. He was pale and nervous. He
hadn't wanted to meet me, either. He was a freshman at Harvard
and was having trouble getting to know girls, my mother told
me. I was to be nice, I was to be friendly. I was to help this boy
because his brother mattered to my cousin Roy who was
important to my father's financial prospects. The waiter hovered.
I took out a cigarette and blew smoke into the air. The boy took
out his cigarette and blew smoke into the air. And I talked to
him. It wasn't easy. He was not happy. I tried sports, books,
classes. What did he like, what were his professors like, what
were the names of his friends, what house did he live in at
Harvard?

There was a rustling in the room as women in hats and veils, in black high heels arrived with red lips and gold earrings. I thought I could smell my own sweat rising from my body to mix with the perfumes in the air. Still I talked. He didn't much, this boy. Then the waiter came to our table with a silver ice bucket and a bottle of champagne. The waiter gestured a few tables away and there was David Schine with Roy Cohn. They were watching the little brother on his date. David Schine was over six feet tall and blond and muscular and looked like a model for men's clothes. David Schine was glistening with youth and money and power and the advantage of perfect teeth. Under the table I scratched at the scab on my knee until it bled.

I DID NOT then think of the two men in bed together. I did think of the poor younger brother, such a shadow of his glamorous older sibling. I tried harder. It was my obligation to my family. The room was dark, the mirror behind the bar was indifferent to what it saw. I had read Mary McCarthy. I wanted to run for my life—I wanted to catch the next wagon leaving for the plains. I wanted to live in a log cabin and love a man who would bring dinner home in a sack on his back, dinner he had killed in the woods. I wanted to escape but instead I talked on to David Schine's little brother. I asked about his stamp collection. Did he like jazz? Did he dance? The answer was no. I had just read The Communist Manifesto in history class. I thought it best not to mention that. Our teacher had said that the ends must never justify the means. Holding to that principle was the basis of all democracy and all moral behavior. But what if you could save a hundred lives by killing three Nazis? You should kill them even though murder was hardly an acceptable means. It was confusing. What if you were sitting on a restaurant terrace in Geneva and at the next table sat a man who owned a diamond mine? He was drinking beer with a business contact. He made his workers sick and paid them badly and allowed mine accidents to kill them as he saved money on repairs. If I had a vial of poison in my pocket should I have poured it into his drink when he went to answer a phone call or should I not?

I was at a time in life when death was a theoretical problem, the possibility of remaining unloved, real as pain itself.

Nevertheless I wanted to remain for all eternity at a table at Schrafft's with my friends and sip my black-and-white soda through a straw and talk about the other girls in my class who were not at the table. Schrafft's had little doilies with cut-out lace patterns. Schrafft's had waitresses in black uniforms and white aprons. Schrafft's had chicken sandwiches with the crusts removed. Schrafft's had sodas and sundaes and old ladies who went there with their companions after their doctor appointments. They rested their canes on the back of their chairs.

If Roy Cohn had been permitted to love David Schine in the open would he have become the Roy Cohn who had young boys brought to his bed as he lay dying of AIDS in Walter Reed Hospital? I think perhaps you needed to come of age in the 1950s to understand how shame rode the commuter trains, rustled in the school halls, spread from person to person as if it were polio, paralyzing as it went.

1954: The God that failed was communism, although all
through my life gods have failed, risen, and failed again. We are
gathered in the community lounge in my house at Sarah
Lawrence where I am a transfer student, a sophomore, watching
the Army–McCarthy hearings on a very small black-and-white
TV set. I am praying for a defeat for Roy Cohn and his boss. I
know that there are impure connections between David Schine
and Roy Cohn. My thoughts are not about sex but about
connections. I know all about connections, how they get you
into clubs and schools and jobs with advantages. I know that
knowing the right people turned a mountain into a hill, a chasm
into a creek. I know that the Rosenbergs, the tragic Rosenbergs,
knew all the wrong people. I know, because my mother told me,
that Judge Al Cohn, Roy's father, was a good man deeply grieved
at the misuse of power indulged in so theatrically by his son. I
know that the son himself was born of a loveless union.

The story my mother told me was that Roy Cohn's father
came from a poor immigrant family who had barely survived in
far-off Flatbush and their American-born son had gone to City
College School of Law and had a great love of his country and
wanted to serve as a judge, a public servant, a bearer of the
weight of democracy, a defender of the Constitution. After his
graduation he went to a bank in the Bronx where the president
of the bank, seeing him waiting in the lobby, took him into his
office, listened to his dreams, took him home for dinner to meet
his daughter Dora, who was, my mother said, the ugliest girl in
all of the Bronx and probably the state. She looked like a

gnome, dwarfish and gnarled. Did she have a hunchback or was that just some memory of mine, merging fairy tales with reality? She had a mean look in her eye, and a mouth my mother said was full of snakes. A judgeship cost a good deal of money: the poor lawyer could never have afforded it but his future father-in-law could. And so a bargain was struck. Roy Cohn, who had no love of little liberties or major freedoms, was the only child of this devil's bargain. So the personal is political and the political takes very personal turns. How else do you learn how the world works except by dragging secrets out of those who know them?

Out in Nevada bombs were tested in the desert and the people who lived in the nearby towns were drinking milk that was glowing in the dark. Later I heard about one little boy who became a real dwarf and other children suffered strange maladies, spines that crumpled, legs that were missing bones. Screenwriters and novelists fled to England. The Communists purged the Jews in their midst. The Americans seemed to be hunting down artists and denying them a living. I am not equating the two on some moral scale, just observing that the politics of fear crossed borders and no one would have been surprised if a real bomb had fallen on our heads, irradiated our crops, and left the world for the fish to take another billion years to struggle onto land and start the process over again. "Stay where you are," I would have yelled at the fish. I myself believed that Machiavellian Roy Cohn was the prince of darkness and McCarthy his king, but where was the promised land and who would take me there?

The witch hunt ended as witch hunts tend to do after a few

burnings at the stake. Roy Cohn went on to make piles of money in a law practice that skirted the legal again and again. He was a celebrity of sorts. He had big parties with famous guests every News Year's eve and my aunt, my mother's sister, was always proud to attend. But the truth was there for all to see—he was a moral dwarf, a quisling to democracy, a man who could not say the name of his loves. This last was not his fault. If only he had crusaded against hypocrisy instead of communism.

Maybe it is true that he and Cardinal Spellman and J. Edgar Hoover had sex together in drag in the back rooms of St. Patrick's parish house. The rumor was all over town. I'm sure that babies in their strollers knew the story. Maybe it is not true. But what is certain is that money and power and dark secrets passed between these men and of these three the most dangerous was probably money, which lifted from honest work, separated from need, becoming a thing in itself that brings power if not understanding, money was the real God that failed us, a God that could not save Roy Cohn from himself.

1956: In the West End Bar I read Donald's poems. I knew he was a true poet because the poems made me tremble. I knew that I wanted to put my body between him and his acute nervous antennae. I wanted to puff him up and give him my courage. Beside him I felt like an insensitive football player warming up for the game. I kept copies of his poems in the hip pocket of my jeans. He was attracted to suicide and death. Like

Rimbaud, he intended to die young. Why was not a question I asked. When was something I worried about.

Each time I walked into the West End Bar and saw that he was sitting on his favorite stool in the middle of the left side of the bar I felt a pressure lift from my chest.

And then after I had been at the bar almost every evening for about three weeks I saw Jack Richardson sitting next to Donald. The now-distant past.

They speak of love at first sight. I don't believe in it. But perhaps at that moment some God laughed unkindly. This was the same Jack I had met at a dance and forgotten all about, so this was love at second sight. Or you could say it was fated to be. Or you could say lightning can strike twice in the same place and eventually it burns the ground to a crisp.

I have always wondered why mountain climbers do it. What is the necessity to make yourself cold and weary, oxygen deprived and footsore, just to get to the top of some fossils, minerals, wormy soil, all piled up in jagged shapes, rock sheers and deep drops that care nothing for human endeavors, passions, reproductive urges? But my first love was like that, dangerous, reason abandoned, sense tossed away, and compulsion driving thought. I was going to climb that mountain, plant a flag on the top, and tumble down the other side.

Donald introduced us. Jack was more than six feet tall and a shank of his black hair hung over his high forehead. He was thin and his lips were pale. He smoked a Gauloises which he waved in his left hand like a conductor's baton as he talked. He was an admirer of T. S. Eliot and Balzac. He believed in nothing but logic, nothing but the beauty of pure reason, which was a thing unto itself, he explained to me, not referring to any reality at all.

He was a student at Columbia on a veteran's scholarship. He had started at the School of General Studies but had made his way into the Philosophy Department at the university. He spoke with a strange British upper-class accent that he had taught himself, having been raised in Queens by his single mother and his grandmother who worked at a store for large ladies on Fifth Avenue and so was able to support her daughter and grandson in a one-bedroom apartment a half a block away from the rattling el, the el that rushed past on the web of steel tracks and support columns, casting the street below in constant streaks of darkness.

Jack asked the bartender for another scotch straight up and he asked me if I could pay for it. I could. Was I interesting? Was I appealing to him? I'm not sure. I was flushed with effort. Starry-eyed with hope. I was aware that he looked at other girls in the bar, aware that Donald felt I was ignoring him, aware that Donald wished Jack would prefer men to women, aware that most people spoke in sentences while Jack Richardson spoke in pages, in paragraphs, perfectly formed, with beginnings and middles and ends, with embellishments and clauses and subclauses. As the bar closed at four in the morning and the garbage trucks came rumbling down Broadway I offered to drive Jack home so he wouldn't have to take the subway. He curled his long frame into my car. He talked about André Malraux and the Ballets Russes. As we drove across the Fifty-ninth Street Bridge with the lights of a tugboat moving across the water beneath us, he told me that he intended to be a great writer, not simply a published writer, not simply a writer who has a small reputation during his lifetime and is forgotten the minute his coffin closes. He wanted to be an immortal writer. His ambition made my stomach turn. What if he failed? There was, he explained to me, no point to breathing in and out, no savior to watch the process, no reforms of the human spirit possible, just words and if the words went without applause, if they fell like our bodies dead into the earth, he would prefer extinction to the tedium of crawling through the monotony that would follow failure.

He wanted a hamburger. His head hurt. We stopped at a White Castle on the Queens side of the bridge. The electric light was flat, and like a police station the restaurant spoke of crimes, only these would be crimes of the soul, cowardly retreats, poverty, and too much Clorox on the bathroom floor. The other customers were sobering up or getting ready to go to work. "I am a logical positivist," he said. I had never met one before. I wasn't quite sure what that was. He explained in great circling sentences that he would only accept theories that could be proved. That speculation was for romantics. His philosophy was hard-edged, unforgiving, dependent on reason and evidence. It contained no explanations of human existence. His hands shook as he spoke to me while we waited for the burgers in their thin stale buns to arrive with a plastic envelope of ketchup on the side. I should have laughed. I should have noticed the pale blue veins throbbing in his high forehead and the odd way he was rocking on the stool. I should have run out the door and left him there some ten blocks from his apartment house and followed the el back to the bridge and returned to Sarah Lawrence weary but intact. Instead like moth to star I eagerly anticipated the singeing of my wings.

I took him home and he left me in the car to drive myself back to college. I came back to the West End Bar the next night and the one after that. Soon it was clear that I would drive him home whenever he liked, and I would buy the drinks and I would bring the cigarettes and I would hope that he would remember me, sitting there.

On my car radio Frank Sinatra sang "Old Devil Moon" and my fingers drummed on the steering wheel. Ella Fitzgerald sang "You like tomato and I like tomahto . . . Let's call the whole thing off." I didn't want to call anything off. I was just getting started.

Somewhere the future members of the SDS and the Weather Underground were storing up grudges against the popular girls, the jocks. Somewhere Louis Armstrong purred through the night and somewhere Bessie Smith was denied hospital care when she had a car accident in the South. I thought America was the real wasteland, never mind what T. S. Eliot had to say. Besides, he was an anti-Semite but so was Dickens and Henry James and Shakespeare. I was accustomed to the fact that genius had its moral imperfections.

Somewhere my mother was lying in her bed, packs of ice over her eyes to stop the swelling caused by the tears she shed night after night because my father had a mistress who had a child by him and he cherished as best he could his mistress not his wife.

I read *Franny and Zooey* and thought it was brilliant although someone had to explain to me that Franny was pregnant. I thought she was just having a religious experience. I was reading *Crime and Punishment*. The professor had said there would be no civilization without guilt. I believed in guilt and put away the childish toys of absolution, forgiveness, the unrealistic wish for mercy. Someone was thinking up the twist, the beginnings of rock and roll. I was humming along as I drove to the West End Bar, "Dancing cheek to cheek." If I had put my ear to the ground, Indian scout–style, I might have heard the sixties coming. I might have heard the feet boarding ships headed to Vietnam. I was nineteen years old and I should have known better but Swann loved Odette and I loved Jack and it seemed to me normal enough.

Joseph Campbell taught a course at Sarah Lawrence that was adored by most students. It was about the hero and myth. It was very Jungian. It had a mystic coating that I distrusted. I quit the course. The girls who loved it best were bent on becoming social workers and I wanted something else. Even Martin Buber—many of my classmates were enamored of Martin Buber (who believed in the "I" and the "thou")—who must have been as sweet as they come, couldn't provide me with what I needed. I wanted to find out why everyone in the *New Yorker* stories I read like sacred texts seemed to float in gray air, destined to a purgatory of one disappointment or another. Was that the way it really was?

In America we didn't really have upper and lower classes. At least it was impolite to notice that one person's parents had trophies from the Harvard wrestling team on their shelves and another person's parents had a framed reproduction of a Madonna and child above a candlelit shrine on a dresser. The clothes one wore, the crookedness of one's teeth, the accent of one's English all gave it away. We were on ladders climbing, striving. It wasn't so simple as this land is your land. It was more watch out, I'm right behind you closing in, or I'm so far above you a little kick would send you tumbling down. From sea to shining sea there was a lot of pushing going on.

And then there was absurdity. The word means ridiculous, without sense, comical without humor. Absurdity was what Jean-Paul Sartre believed was real. The only reality for galaxies near and far. Absurdity was what Samuel Beckett knew was the only dependable truth in a world made of curved mirrors in which all men were clowns. Absurdity was what Jean Genet knew was what happened when you went to prison. Absurdity was what the world looked like if you removed God from the center of your thoughts. It was what followed like a hangover after a binge if you began to think of space and time and the smallness of the human endeavor and the absence of a moral center to things.

Absurdity was very fashionable. I believed in it with all my heart. It was a shortcut way of saying that the world had no moral order. It was a winking way of saying that I belonged to the world of philosophers and shared the current despair. I did. It meant I would drink coffee in Café Renzi in Greenwich Village and read Auden poems in the dentist's office while waiting to have my cavity filled. It meant that my mind was so full of words that I couldn't see where I was going. Which is why when the moon was already disappearing over the river and the stars had turned pale and the lights of the Nabisco factory glowed like dying fireflies against the dawn I was often driving Jack across the Fifty-ninth Street Bridge, parking the car in the street while he wrote things in his notebook, waiting while he ate his last bite at the White Castle.

At the West End Bar we formed a group. There was Donald, and Peter, who would become a famous minimalist painter, and Morris, who would become the bold light of the classical music world. There was tall and bone-thin Serena, who was the daughter of a Brooklyn longshoreman and had long black hair and dark black eyes and a way of looking at you that conveyed a desire to punch your teeth in. There was little Judith, who was the daughter of refugees and a blond-haired boy, who wanted to make a movie of us as we moved about in our clouds of smoke up and down the bar. There was Luke who had dropped out of high school and was living in the back of his father's car, which he had stolen and parked on a street in Harlem. He cadged cigarettes and sandwiches and a drink or two, and in return he drew on a napkin a sketch of something. I kept the napkins in the back of my notebook. And on the other side of the horseshoe bar the engineers and the mathematicians and the chemistry types were gathered, eyeing us with contempt, or was it envy?

C. P. Snow was soon to say that the worlds of art and science were too distant from each other. He would soon notice that the two great intellectual endeavors of the human mind weren't talking. We didn't think it dangerous that we were split apart: those with a predilection for fact and those with a leaning toward fantasy. We thought they were dull and destined to a drab future. They thought we were mad, headed for skid row, failure, the loony bin, the trash basket. They carried slide rules and compasses. We carried worn copies of *The Iliad* and *The Inferno*, and some of us like Jack could recite Auden poem after poem, his memory never fading despite the scotch, despite the late hour, despite the fact that after a while even the people on our side of the bar stopped listening and drifted into their own conversations in which Auden had no part.

Was C. P. Snow right? Should the scientists have listened to Auden and should the poets have learned to use a slide rule? If each of us were allowed two minds, a second life, a brain that could serve two masters, that would have been fine but in the West End Bar we were one or the other. I held the scientists responsible for the crematoria and the trains that carried the children to their deaths. I held the scientists responsible for splitting an atom that might better have retained its original unity. We thought they had no souls. They thought we had no brains. Their world flourished in order and cleanliness. Ours sought out the darkness, the upside downness of those who knew, really knew that the abyss waited. They didn't care much one way or the other. We cared and talked about the God we did not believe in all the time. We spoke to Him angrily, nastily, pleading, posing, begging, mocking.

And one night I walked to the other side of the bar on my way to a friend in a back booth and as I walked past an engineering student he said something flirty to me. I smiled at him. Stay here, he said to me, making room at the bar. I shook my head, no. He put his hand on my arm. Just to stall me, just to get me to stay a minute longer, but from the other side of the bar came a voice: "Get your hands off of her." And that is the way it began. No surprise to C. P. Snow what happened next.

When I remember this I do not think of myself as Helen of Troy. When I remember this I think of my cowardice. I had never hit anyone, or bit anyone. I cried easily and when tense I bit my thumb, my own thumb. I was a girl who had been taught to curtsey when meeting an adult. I was a girl who spoke about the genius of Hobbes and the foolishness of Rousseau but who believed deep down that love, my rising inchoate, desperate love, could make a garden out of a graveyard. I believed smiling helped.

Girls in my class at Smith College had been pinned to their fraternity boys and would marry them within a year. My new friends at Sarah Lawrence were spending weekends at Yale with boys they would become pregnant by and marry before graduation. It wasn't as if we had time to make a mistake and correct it later. Youth was fleeing as fast as it could. At nineteen the finish line was in sight.

And so I was sitting in the West End Bar, in my leotard, still trying to inhale my cigarette without coughing. America was the land of the free, so we had been told in school, but what was one free to do? To marry well, to tend the garden, to bring the child here and there in a station wagon? If communism was the God that failed, if socialism was the God that turned into a clown, if there was no place to dress in knight's armor and show the king's colors, then what was to be done? If all around the important things were secret, who slept with whom, who loved whom, who passed out in the bathroom, who hated his wife, what wife would put her head in the oven next, then what was to be done?

Of course someone might write a play, a novel, a poem and the written word itself would provide a parachute, a way to escape.

What happened next? An engineer came to our side of the bar and Jack said something unkind about his limited brain and someone smashed someone in the nose and the blood flowed onto his shirt and someone picked up a bottle and knocked Jack on the head and opened a chasm in his scalp and his dark black hair turned red and someone screamed and all the men except Donald were leaping into a pile and slide rulers became weapons and beer bottles crashed to the ground and Serena jumped on the bar and standing high threw salt shakers, forks, and glasses at the enemy and it was clear that war had begun, war between the poets and the artists and the technocrats who would build us air conditioners and refrigerators and whose imagination ran to square roots and multiples of pi. Those with Euripides in mind, with Virgil ranting in the background, with Rilke sighing and Proust gasping for breath in his cork-lined room, with Plato watching the shadows in the cave, those of us who didn't follow football seemed to be at a disadvantage. I thought that my heroes had shown their true colors. We had caused a battle between art and technology, a struggle between those who had brought us the A-bomb and Zyklon-B and those who wrote poetry on napkins. I was frozen in my spot. The

police came and each side claimed the other had started it and
there was blood on my shoes and blood on my hands and I took
Jack to the St. Luke's emergency room to have his scalp sewn
together. I had discovered that I was a coward. I was not capable
of attack. My arms had hung at my sides. My eyes had seen
everything but my legs did not move. I drove Jack back to
Queens that night and in the car my love raged and billowed out
over the entire city. He had stitches in his head. He had stitches
on his hand, his beautiful hand with his long fingers flying in
the air. I had tried to clean my leotard with club soda and it was
damp and still stained. Jack talked about the Trojan War, about
Aeneas and Achilles and the urge of men toward war and death.
He talked again about his own death—the death that would
come by his own hand. The thought of his death, the thought of
losing him made me frantic. I would help him. I would not let
that happen. I would save him, how I wasn't sure, but as we
pulled up to his apartment building and the steel armature of
the el loomed above us and the street was stilled in the new
morning's light and in the distance an ambulance wailed I knew
what my life's work would be. I would save him.

I WROTE A PIECE for the Sarah Lawrence newspaper. It was
a challenge to the president of the college, Harold Taylor, who
was asking all his students to find their identity. Where, where, I
asked, is it hiding, under the bed? Harold Taylor was married
and his wife wore beautiful flowered dresses when she greeted
the students invited into their home. Gossip had it that Harold

Taylor's wife drank more than her share of the liquid refreshments offered at presidential affairs.

I did not like Simone Weil because she added another death to the Nazi count when it wasn't necessary. I wanted to be at least four inches taller. Jack had told me I was too short and he admired tall blond women with long straight hair. This did not alter my feelings for him. I admired tall blond women with long straight hair too. I just wasn't one of them.

I understand this is puzzling. It has a name in the psychiatric manuals: masochism. As with all labels it is true, but just the beginning of truth. Under the label lay love, my first deep love, and it was for the mind of an artist, a mind far better than mine, more dazzling, extended into the disciplines of philosophy, poetry, history. Also a mind more desperate, more drunk, more in pain than I was, a magnetic force, a gravitational pull to another sphere, a passion that even as I know better, even as I now regret it, was not without its own grandeur.

AT FIRST IT WAS just the small white buds on the trees that lined the highway back from the Upper West Side to Bronxville where the campus of Sarah Lawrence sat, a suburban country club, a beehive of female expectation, some of us star-crossed, destined for mental hospitals, psychiatrist offices before we began, others headed for lives as amateur cellists, or Sunday-afternoon painters, or members of their local museum's board of trustees. A moment later it was spring in bloom, apple trees with pink flowers, daffodils on the side of the exit road, warm air that made me keep the top down on the car and let the dawn sit on my shoulders as I drove back from Queens, racing the early-morning dew to the gates of the college.

Then one night I arrived at the bar to find Jack already there, a drink in his hand, his face ashen, his hand holding his cigarette trembling. There were dark shadows under his eyes. This was not his first drink of the evening. I paid the tab to the bartender. Jack announced to all of us that he had not received the Konrad Adenauer fellowship he had counted on to take him to Europe in June. Despite the recommendations of the Philosophy Department at Columbia he had been turned down. "There is nothing for me to do," he said, "I am finished before I have begun." A crack like the ones that appear in a broken plate traveled down my chest. Everyone offered encouragement, everyone said the decision was a sign of German stupidity. Everyone was subdued as if someone had died. Someone in fact was in danger of dying. Like a great bird shot in mid-flight Jack draped himself across the bar and his dark hair fell in his eyes and he said he was done, done with living. I bought more drinks. I drove him home. I tried to suggest other options, but what? There was no money for graduate school. His grandmother's job would provide no extra funds. His mother had died. His father occasionally played the piano in a local bar and lived off the royalties of a song he had composed, "I don't want her, You can have her, She's too fat for me," or something like that. "You could write at home," I said. "I can't," he said. "We'll think of a way," I said as the dark water shimmered with the lights of the passing tugboat that was approaching the bridge. I was thinking of stealing my mother's pearl necklace and using the money to buy Jack a year abroad, a year to write words that I knew would last a thousand years into the future, words that would surely be worth the price of a pearl necklace. And when he staggered off into his apartment building and I turned back toward Manhattan, I felt a grief for him as deep as the river itself.

Two days later I arrived at the West End Bar to see Jack talking about the pagan rites that survived into Christianity, his eyes alight, his hands flying about to emphasize his point, his long sentences wrapping themselves like coiled ropes on a boat on the open seas. Yes, he had received the fellowship. The money was generous. He would go to Germany after all. But he had been turned down, but no he had not, he had just anticipated it, practiced it, wanted to see how it would be if he were rejected. He had the money. My mother's pearl necklace was safe in her black velvet jewelry box. I was less safe. I forgave him for the crack in my chest. I understood he was simply frightened. If I could have protected him from that fright I would have.

Someone else might have been angry. I'm sure someone was. I felt only relief. Artists have permission to do the unthinkable because they cannot be bound by our rules. Prometheus brought us the fire of the gods and there's no sense in asking Prometheus to obey the traffic laws.

Eleanor Roosevelt spoke at my graduation. Almost all of us had declared on our college applications that she was the woman we most admired. What we may have meant is that she was the woman whose name we knew who had not been an

international spy, was not a fashion designer or a movie star. Her
photo was not on the engines of war planes. We did not know
her breast size. Her toothy mouth seemed to prove that she had
escaped the orthodontist. This was virtue enough for me.

Many of my Jewish classmates had little noses, little
upturned noses. These were the product of the plastic surgeons
trade in social insecurity, in capitulation to the images in fashion
magazines. Blood and stitches, bandages and bruises all borne
without complaint. The fulfillment of a desire to be not so
Jewish as all that. These little noses sat in faces that hardly
recognized themselves in the mirror, faces with a strange
expression, a questioning look: Who am I, am I fooling you?

Of course I too knew about the pyramid of American life. I
too understood that at the top of it all a certain Protestant sat,
fourth generation of lawyers in the family, five generations at
Harvard, six generations at Andover, seven generations since the
first member of the family to arrive brought his library off the
boat in boxes. I too understood that while words about equality
were everywhere, some clubs would have you and some would
not. And Jack, Jack could move like a panther across the social
stage and go anywhere he wished. His upper-class nearly British
accent was fake, but a brilliant fake. I intended not to be
impressed by his success as an imposter. But perhaps I imagined
a social ladder let down from heaven just for him and I believed
that it would be sensible to put my foot on the first rung and
begin to climb at his side.

I also believed that I should go work in Appalachia and
teach poetry to children without shoes.

1957: It turned out that Jack's fellowship started on September 1. I was going to Paris for the second time with a group of girls and we planned to go to Florence to study art. That is what my mother understood. Jack could not come to Paris with me because he did not have the money and his fellowship only began in September and so I went to a cousin of mine, a daredevil of a cousin who wore a tapestry vest to the opera and kept a closetful of women's dresses in his apartment and was seen with men in ways that made my mother shudder with horror. This cousin of mine was the son of the owner of a large paper business, miles of forest, a town in their name existed in Vermont. The money to him would mean nothing and to me it was everything just then. And so I called him and came to his apartment. I couldn't say just what I needed it for. I was afraid he would tell my mother. I hinted instead that I needed to end a pregnancy. I hinted that it was a life and death matter. He asked me to pay it back. It was $500. Jack bought a ticket on a boat to Paris and we planned to meet at an apartment I would rent.

All right—I know there is a great lack of dignity in this gift I gave Jack. Shame rises as I think of this financial exchange. Is there a defense? Did I purchase my own fate?

I UNDERSTOOD Thomas Mann very well. Tonio Kröger, who was the hero of the novel, was dark, born of an Italian mother, an outsider to the blond fair German culture. Hans, the boy he admired, was the perfect Aryan, at ease with girls, a leader among the boys, and Tonio was shy, awkward, thoughtful,

not an athlete. Tonio was an artist, he was an outsider and he
was doomed to suffer. Did I grasp the homoerotic vibrations of
Tonio for Hans? I don't remember. What I did grasp was that the
artist, the writer, was an eye looking in at the window of
another's happiness, another's complacent existence, and that
the artist was separated from normal human happiness by his
temperament, by his quick mind, by the oddness of his soul,
by the gifts that would allow him to observe and create. I might
have thought Tonio Kröger was a sorrowful figure. I might have
pictured myself at the dancing class waltzing with Hans—of
course by the time I read the story I knew that Hans would have
been more than willing to throw me on a train headed for my
graveless grave. It was also clear that scotch and bourbon, rye
and whiskey, straight or with ice, was the lubricant of art, as
important as the brush to the painter, as important as words to the
writer. Only jazz musicians took drugs. It wasn't that everyone
else was cautious or uninterested. But the bar was open and men
drank and writers drank more and no one I knew thought of this
as a disease, no one intervened to prevent anyone else's thirst. A
dry writer was to be pitied. Where did he hang out, who were his
companions, how did he ease himself through the day? The
assumption here is that writers needed more easing than
bankers, that writers were entitled to more easing because they
suffered the nicks of the heart so much more deeply.

And then there was *Doctor Faustus*. Thomas Mann had
written a book about a composer who made a pact with the devil
and became a great composer. The syphilis he had contracted as
a young man may have produced the illusion of Mephistopheles

or perhaps Mephistopheles arranged for the young composer to be entranced and entrapped by a whore named Esmeralda who gives him the disease that in the end destroys his brain and his gift. Of course this was about Nazi Germany and its man-made fires of hell that consumed all around. But Thomas Mann appeared to be saying that the devil lived in art, perhaps because humans who create challenge God at His own game. I believed that Faustus had made the right bargain: anything, anything at all for art. This was a religious belief temptingly disguised as an antireligious belief. It was romantic in the worst sense of the word. It was not about tender human moments but about great storms blowing apart the order of things. I was a romantic although I would have denied it had anyone thought to accuse me of such an unfashionable state of mind.

Salinger had withdrawn to New Hampshire. Was he drinking there? John O'Hara was always in bars, at least in his fiction. Liquor was flowing like print. There were AA meetings across the country but I don't believe there was a central office to call to find the nearest one. Dylan Thomas died in a New York hospital after watering his liver with alcohol for days on end. Dorothy Parker was a drunk. Most of those at the Algonquin roundtable drank their lunch. I thought of drinking the way I now think of gas you put in the car. You get to a place where it is available, you pour it into the opening intended for it, and your car will go for miles until it needs more. I thought of gas not as a diminishing commodity, not as the oil companies' exclusive hold on our economy, or the environment's flirtation with destruction. I thought of it as the substance that makes the automobile move: so I thought scotch and soda, its beautiful amber color, its place in a glass sliding down the bar toward some eager hand, was just the normal way of things, the lubricant of art, its mundane grain-brewed muse. Too bad it tasted so awful.

So one night at the West End Bar we all decided to go to a party at Esther's apartment. Her parents were away. Someone brought a bag with bottles of hard liquor. We were sitting on their couch. I could see Hebrew books in the shelves. I could see in Esther's black sad eyes the stories that lived in that apartment. And then I saw Jack lope over to Esther and take her hand and lean down to her small round face and stroke her hair. Then I saw Jack whispering in her ear and then I saw them both disappear into her bedroom down the hall. And then I reached for the scotch and I had one and then another and then another and then I grew faint and lay on the floor and then I forget what happened next except that some friends delivered me, barely standing, smelling of vomit, blacked out, erased, to my mother's door at two in the morning. I told her I had eaten bad Chinese food. She did not believe me. I was sick for another day, my head pounding, my heart skipping beats, and aching with Jack's betrayal and whatever else was pinching my arteries, rushing heedlessly through my valves. Thank God, Jack was not in my car when he started flirting with Esther because I might have driven the vehicle right into a cement wall. Anger can be like that, a boomerang making a precision turn.

But Esther had no car to drive Jack home to Queens at

night. Esther had no money to pay for his drinks. Esther was
forgotten quickly. If ever there was a pyrrhic victory, this was it.

1964: Larry Rivers or a friend of his wrote a play or was it
a "happening." It was performed in the backyard of the house I
rented in Amagansett that summer. I have forgotten the plot. I
think it had no plot. It was about sex, however. Many panels of
curtains waved in the breeze. We had set up chairs in the yard.
There was a lot of drinking and the child stayed up. There were
flashlights instead of spotlights and pratfalls and laughter and the
improvised lines were sometimes incoherent. It didn't matter. A
wonderful time was had by all.

That was the summer I released into the wild the black-and-
white rabbit I had bought for the child. It had eaten all the glue
on my caned chairs. It had eaten the binding of the French
books in the lower shelves of the bookcase and there was no way
to explain to a rabbit that control of bladder and bowel is a
sanitary matter. The rabbit was called Alouette. The child loved
the rabbit. I convinced her it would be happier in the wild
bushes behind the house. I thought it would be eaten by the first
raccoon it met. Nevertheless during the play I watched for the
rabbit to reappear. I was hoping it would be attracted by the lights
or the noise in the yard. However, we never saw Alouette again.

1957: In the apartment I rented on boulevard du
Montparnasse there was a two-burner stove, a sink, and a bed

and large windows overlooking the street. There was a desk
where Jack's typewriter sat. Across the street there was a small
café bar and the waiters put out tables in the early morning. Jack
woke around noon and I would fix him some coffee on our
electric appliance and then he would go out to the bar and sit
on the stool and have a *pain au chocolat* and he would return
and sometimes he worked on a short story and sometimes he
went into the small closet that was near the bed and he would
take a hanger from the bar and shake his arms up and down, the
hanger moving up and down as if he were shaking the dust out
of a blanket. He would move his arms so the hanger would pass
before his blinking eyes again and again. He needed to do this,
he said. Sometimes he needed to do this for hours on end. Yes, I
knew this was not usual. I had never seen anyone else shake a
hanger up and down in fast rhythmic motions. I had never read
about anyone shaking a hanger up and down. It seemed to
soothe him. No one was harmed while he was in the closet
behind closed doors shaking his arms. Years later I saw a film of
an autistic child shaking his hands in front of his face in just the
same way. Years later I understood this was more than an
idiosyncrasy. It was a disaster of neuron and nerve, synapse and
protein, stirred in a cocktail of the mind, worse than absinthe,
worse than mushrooms, worse than cocaine, a poison brewed in
the frantic soul. Somewhere nearby Simone de Beauvoir was
fixing Jean-Paul breakfast. Somewhere nearby surviving leaders
of the small Resistance were writing their memoirs of a time
when every minute of life counted because one expected so few
of them. Years before Isadora Duncan had taken a lover in a

hotel on the corner and Zelda, mud on her silver shoes, a run in her hose, hair askew, ran down the middle of the street shouting for Scott who was somewhere else tying one on. On to what, who can say.

In Paris: A man sat down to talk to me at the corner bar. He is the son of a famous violinist who played first violin for the Berlin Orchestra before the war. He was Jewish and the family fled to Cuba and everything they had was lost, including the violin. The man I was talking to tells me that when he was a child he sat on his grandfather's knee in a park in Berlin and several religious Jews from the east came by, children, women, men in fur-trimmed hats, and his grandfather said to him, "Those people are at fault. They make the citizens hate us. But for them we would simply be Germans." The man told me that his uncle had a Silver Cross he won in battle in the First World War. His uncle died in Mauthausen. "Are you Jewish?" the stranger asked me. "Yes," I said. "I won't tell anyone," he said. "That will be our secret." He spoke to me in French. "Are you living in France now?" I asked. "No," he said. "I move around from place to place." He kissed me gently on my cheek and walked away. A car honked its horn. Three schoolgirls wearing uniforms and carrying books came dashing past. I was sitting in a café and standing at the edge of a grave at the same time. It is not mourning I felt but rather panic. Murder was in the air.

Jack talks over his ideas for stories with me. I offer suggestions. I admire each sentence. His work is brilliant. The sentences swing into the atmosphere, they riff on Hegel, they alight on Kierkegaard. They occasionally move the plot forward. They speak to me of the emptiness of the heavens and the ungodliness of the earth. I retype his pages so they are clean. It takes a long time. I write my mother a postcard about the wonders of the Louvre. I write to my cousin who loaned me the money that Paris is fine and so am I. The first part of that sentence was true. I am lonely at night. Jack leaves at dusk and most often doesn't return until dawn. He tells me that he has to do this. He needs the night streets. He needs the prostitutes up on the hill. He needs a lot of money each evening. I understand. But at night as I sit in the bed and make my way through Thomas Mann's *Joseph and His Brothers* I am uneasy, as if I am very small and the room very large: neither of which was true. I don't ask myself why Jack isn't with me or me with him. I don't ask myself why he doesn't touch me under the covers when he finally returns to our apartment, his gait unsteady, his eyes red, his hands flying about erratically. I am in Paris, living with a writer, a writer who will be famous one day, who will write things to astonish the world, will make the emptiness of life full with his descriptions and vibrate with his words, or so I think, or so I think I think. Outside my window I hear men and women laughing talking in the street, arm in arm, they are moving past my window, I listen carefully. That is the sound of Paris at midnight.

JACK CONSIDERS SENDING one or two of his stories out to small literary magazines. I encourage him. He says he will kill himself if they are rejected. I do not believe they will be rejected. I believe in him with all my being. I gather the pages. I go to the post office and buy an envelope. I go to the bookstore and look up the addresses of a few of the better publications. No, he says, don't send them. I will write other better ones. I wait. One day he will have to let me send them out.

I burn the hot plate. I don't remember how. I tear a curtain in my effort to open a window. Jack stains the table with a broken wine bottle. I cut myself on the glass as I try to pick it up from the floor. The summer moves on. In the fall Jack will go to Munich on his Adenauer fellowship. I want to go with him. I think he wants me to go. I will need my winter coat. Did Jack want me to go with him? I think he did. I will have to explain this to my mother. I write her. She writes me back: "Get married." Jack says, "Why not get married? We don't have to take it seriously." I will need my winter coat.

My father flies to Paris and goes with us to city hall in the fourteenth (or maybe it was the sixteenth) arrondissement. The mayor who marries us says that he has never had a divorce in his district so we are a lucky couple. I feel guilty right then, standing in front of him in my flowered dress with a white rose in my hair. I have a premonition we will be his first divorce. It is the middle of the summer and still a chill comes over me. We go to lunch at Maxim's. My father gives Jack a few hundred dollars for a honeymoon. We are going to Brittany to see the town that Proust had written about as Combray. We are going to the North Sea. But after lunch, after my father leaves, Jack says he needs the money for a few nights on the town by himself. He needs to drink. I understand. He goes off alone on our honeymoon and I wait at the apartment. He comes back four days later, white and shaking. His black hair oily and matted, his skin patchy and red in places. He is hungry and tired and sleeps for hours. I am worried that he is sick but he recovers and a few weeks later we go to Munich.

This was certainly not the wedding my mother would have planned for me. That one would have taken place in the Plaza Hotel. I would have a long white gown. She would wear something gold with lace and glittering beads and a band would play and the guests would dance and the waiters would move about the ballrooms with silver trays and long-stemmed wineglasses. That was the point of my wedding in Paris—a counter-wedding to a man who took the vow with as many grains of salt as it is possible to sprinkle on a vow before it dissolves in a double bourbon on the rocks.

Another cousin of mine comes to Paris with his wife. He is the vice president of the shirt company my grandfather founded. He is handsome and very sweet and wants to take us out to dinner. So there we are having dinner at the Tour d'Argent on the Île de la Cité. Paris sparkles out the window. The silver and the white china, the elaborately folded napkins, the bowing waiters, the gilt chairs all reflected in the mirrors, beside us the Seine flows past. My cousin knows no French so he offers Jack the wine list. Jack speaks at great length to the waiter. We eat dinner. We drink the wine. My worlds have come together. My cousin speaks of discount stores. My cousin's wife speaks of the Louvre and her plans to go to Venice and Jack explains Hegel to my not-so-interested cousin while his white fingers wave about—swans moving across the clear waters. I eat the chocolate mousse with raspberry sauce and drink the dessert wine which comes in a small crystal glass shaped like a rosebud at dawn.

The bill comes. My cousin picks it up. "My God," he says, "that wine was $150. One bottle, $150." Three or was it four empty wine bottles gleam in the candlelight. After my cousin and his wife wave goodbye and we watch their taxi disappear down the street, Jack turns toward Montmartre, a club there, a person he promised to meet, and I walk to our apartment, the duck with orange sauce laying in my gut, a certain feeling of sadness washing over me. It is Paris, I think, that makes me sad, beheadings and revolutions, poems and regrets, women leaning on lampposts waiting for their next man, cigarette smoke rising from the tables of the sidewalk cafés. The wine has made me feel like a small point at the end of a long line, an almost invisible point.

WE HAVE ARRIVED in Munich and rented an apartment on the top floor of a limestone house on Bavariaring. Out my window I see the round park where Hitler spoke to thousands of enthusiasts as Nazi flags waved and arms saluted in the familiar *Sieg Heil* gesture and row upon row of soldiers and civilians roared in approval as their leader promised victory in a war just begun. We had dinner at the Fierjahrzeiten Hotel in the very room that Hitler had taken over for his headquarters. I wrote my name on the cloth napkin in ink. I wrote my name in the mist on the windows in our apartment over and over again. I had a point to make. One morning, alone in the apartment, I heard heavy thudding boots on the stairs. They came closer and closer, rising up floor after floor. Then there was a knock on my door, and I opened the door and I saw knee-high shining black boots and a black jacket and someone with a black hat with an insignia on it was standing there and I passed out at his feet. A fright had taken my breath and I swooned like a heroine in a nineteenth-century novel. The man at the door called for help. My landlady raced up the stairs and someone brought me a wet rag and wiped my face. I returned to consciousness and was much embarrassed to learn that the man in the boots was my postman trying to bring me a special delivery letter from my mother telling me that my winter coat was on the way.

Downstairs in the landlady's apartment I sit at a long table in her dining room. The lady was thin and angular and her gray hair was pulled back in a bun. Behind her is a black-bordered photograph of a handsome middle-aged man in SS uniform. He died, she informed me, at the eastern front. On the wall to the left of her was the photograph, also bordered in black, of her handsome blond son in SS uniform. He died too, in the Ukraine. And then on her right was another photograph bordered in black, her younger son in a pilot's uniform. He died over the Atlantic on his way to England. I looked down at the tea leaves in my cup. And so she said to me, "Where are you from?" "I am from America," I say. "You have my passport in your cupboard." "Yes," she says, "I know, but where are you from?" "New York," I say. "No," she says, "I mean where are your people from?" That is what she wants to know. If I lie I will be a coward and hate myself afterward. If I tell the truth I will make her uncomfortable. I will frighten myself with the unsaid. I will confirm something she suspects. "I am Jewish," I say. "I thought so," she said and got up to clear the tea things away. The light from the windows reflected on the glass of the photographs. The faces of the males in her family blurred. I made my excuses. It was our last tea. She had lonely eyes but I could not ease her loneliness and I never tried.

AT THE UNIVERSITY of Munich Jack meets a graduate student in philosophy from Rhode Island, Barney Randall. He is married to a woman named Nora and they have two children, one and a half and three. They are both in their early twenties. They are Catholics. Nora had been converted in a convent boarding school where her mother had placed her during the war after her father had disappeared in the Pacific and her mother went to work in a department store. Barney and Jack talked philosophy. Nora and I talked about the children. This was the first baby I had changed and the first baby I had bathed. I walked with Nora in the parks and we talked about our childhoods. She was a beautiful girl with glowing black eyes and a curiosity about everything. Barney was always working on his thesis. He also took in English students. One of his students was a hairdresser named Wolf. Wolf had a dark beard and muscular arms and a slight limp in his left leg. Wolf loved the opera and wanted to take Nora to see all the famous landmarks in Munich. He took photographs of railroad stations. He was fascinated with the shadows of the steel grid above and the parallel rails running away from the iron gates. He was planning on moving to

America, that is why he was studying English with Barney. He too thought that America was the land of opportunity. It was the home of the victors whose army still camped on the outskirts of town and whose soldiers walked the streets practicing the German phrase of the day they had heard over the American broadcast station at the end of the morning news program: *Bitte shön Fräulein, will you have a picnic with me?* Wolf wanted to go to the conquerors' hometown and prove himself there. It was Barney's idea that Wolf might improve his English by escorting Nora to movies and cafés and perhaps a museum or two. Barney stayed home, his books spread across the kitchen table, his children sleeping in their small room at the back of the apartment. He was happy for the time to work. He was happy for the peace and quiet.

New Year's eve we have a party at Barney and Nora's apartment. An American biographer and his girlfriend who both have fellowships at the university, a student who is doing his thesis on Thornton Wilder and who has befriended Jack, the downstairs neighbors join us. We are altogether about twenty people. Champagne is cheap. We are rich on deutsche marks. We bring bottles and bottles of champagne. The room is crowded. Just before midnight we bring out the glasses and Barney holds the champagne bottle high in the air. There are shouts of joy. There is the New Year coming toward us, ready or not. And Barney presses down on the bottle neck and the cork explodes outward in a direct line and hits the eye of a man sitting on the couch and the man screams and blood flows and his eye is mangled and his hands are over his eyes and his girlfriend is calling for help. There are no doctors at the party, just literature and philosophy students. The couple leaves for the hospital. His eye is out. Oedipus comes into the conversation. Homer is mentioned. There is blood on the couch. The balloons we have bought bounce against the ceiling but the celebration is over. It is now 1958. Jack leans against the doorway waving his arms as if conducting a secret symphony. The children are awake and staring at the debris from the party.

Shall we go to Dachau? Jack says yes. Barney says yes. I say no. I don't want to go. It is just at the end of town, a little rail trip. I know it's there. I don't want to see it. I go with them. I am quiet. I am numb. I believed it before I saw it. I believe it now. Jack and Barney discuss the nature of human evil. I am quiet. On the trip back I look at the people in the street and I see murderers and children of murderers all bundled up against the cold, their wool scarves protecting their necks, their heavy gloves protecting their fingers, and I see those who wouldn't have seen me in a line marching toward the chambers. I know they smelled it. I know they saw the smoke. Jack and Barney are looking for a place to have a beer. I am suddenly afraid even of Jack and Barney. Do they understand? Not the way I do, they don't. Everyone around speaks German. I wish they didn't.

1958: It is Fasching. In Munich the last week before Lent is a carnival week. There are large masked balls in the museums, in the parks, in the libraries. They are open to the public and it is said that anything you do during Fasching doesn't count

against your soul, it doesn't count against your marriage. It is a
time to be free of the rules. At two in the morning the trolley
runs and the ticket taker picks up the drunks who have passed
out on the streets and the conductors bring them to their
doorsteps. And so Jack leaves me at the ball. I am wearing a
black pussycat mask and a tight shirt. *Nein, danke,* I say over and
over again. The masks and the costumes and the swirling lights
are both exciting and awful, as if the id of the people were
released into the air and lust and lewdness, sin and drunkenness
would never retreat, had tasted victory and would remain abroad
ever after. Everyone is shouting. Everyone is singing loudly.
Everyone is stamping their feet and the music thumps and roars.
I am dizzy, not from drink but from the motion all around me.
Jack disappears. He disappears for five days. It's allowed. I know
that all was forgiven before Christ was lifted to the cross. The
city grew quiet and repentance could be seen in bent heads, in
dark shadows under people's eyes, and the weather grew warmer
and the winds gentle. I knew that sin had been erased from the
souls of the partygoers. Or so they thought. Atone, atone, I
wanted to call out from my window, like some biblical
prophetess I wanted to accuse the passersby of the thing they
weren't thinking about. But what could I threaten them with?
Stores were opening, buildings were rising where rubble had
been. The *wirtschaftswunder* was wonderful. What could I say.
There would be no flood or fire or retribution. Just deutsche
marks gathering in the banks, piling up higher with the passing
days. The church bells rang across the city, the families walked
together in the parks, the little children fed the pigeons, and

Jack and I ate Easter eggs with Barney and Nora on a hill by a lake where ducks paddled.

So who could blame Nora for breaking her vows? So who could blame Wolf for taking advantage of the moment presented? And Nora explained to me that Wolf was a perfect lover while Barney fumbled and breathed heavily but was too fast and too brusque. Nora knew she was sinning but she believed that sins can be forgiven. She assumed that Barney would forgive her when she confessed. He vomited when she told him. He refused to touch her after that. He said that she had violated the place from which his children came and he would never forgive her or touch her again. Now what was she to do? On afternoons I accompanied her on trips to various churches across the city. She had the children in their carriage and sometimes I would lift one or the other in my arms and I would tell them stories while she went into confession to talk to the priest. One after another they urged her to wait and be patient and suffer the punishment her husband offered. Then one rainy afternoon we entered a large cathedral in downtown. The priest had a kind face and he gave the children a little cake and I sat with them in the pews waiting as they spilled crumbs on the floor. This priest told Nora that since she had converted to Catholicism as a young girl she needed twelve or was it fourteen weeks of bridal training and not the more usual number. He said she was entitled to an annulment and he would write to Rome for her and arrange it. She came out of the booth looking ill. We walked across town in silence.

If she could get an annulment on such flimsy grounds then

she felt the entire prohibition against divorce was a farce and she would have nothing to do with Catholicism anymore. She soon packed her bags and took the children and went to New York to live with Wolf who worked as a hairdresser on Madison Avenue and perfected his English very quickly.

THE YEAR IN Munich ends. We return to New York. My mother has furnished an apartment for us. I go to typing class. I go out into the world to find a job. Jack is writing. A literary magazine has taken one of his stories. But several others have rejected him. Each rejection is a reason to go out drinking. He pawns the silver given me by an aunt. He pawns my china. He pawns my gold watch, a high-school graduation gift from my mother. He promises to redeem them when the play he is working on is produced. I talk to my mother on the phone several times a day. I tell her how happy I am. I hope she believes me. I worry. How I am going to have a baby if Jack doesn't touch me? I am always asleep when he comes home. I am out the door hours before he wakes. I see him from a great distance, a cloud of smoke from his cigarette in front of his face. He may not see me at all. I become a good typist.

1961 : I lay my baby on the pile of coats in the bedroom. She is asleep. I hope she will stay asleep as it is hard to hear her over the noise of the party in the next room. We are at George Plimpton's regular Friday-night gathering and the scotch is flowing and the air is filled with smoke and the women are in black silk dresses and the men are like so many crows on a telegraph line looking over the passing scene. Every once in a while one breaks from the group and leans toward a woman, an eager tremble in his smile, a casual holding of her elbow, a kiss to the back of the neck. There is music playing on the Victrola. Is it Ray Charles or is it Ella or Billie Holiday. I see Norman Mailer's curly hair and broad chest. I see a painter who has lost a leg in the Korean War. I see a group around Doc Humes listening as he proposes a writers union that will only sell to the greedy in Hollywood when the price is right for all writers. He says that with a union behind them writers will be able to determine the taste that rules the silver screen. They will not be vassals in an alien kingdom but the rulers themselves, the innermost council. It is a utopian idea. He wants to organize the only American profession whose members believe that brotherhood is a grand ideal for other people, a dreamy concept that forces most writers in the room to nod in agreement while secretly hoping to flee to a private cave and sit in the darkness until the pressure to link arms passes.

I cross my legs and my skirt hikes up over my knees. I spill ashes from my cigarette on the carpet. I see the amber scotch, the darker bourbon, the jar of olives, the white gin, the green vermouth, the silver bucket of ice. One of Plimpton's girls will refill the bucket again and again as the evening moves on. There is a crowd now around Doc Humes. His dark eyes are blazing with the excitement of his brain. I see his wife thumbing through a copy of *The Paris Review* in the corner. She seems unimpressed by his words. There is a wry turn to her lips as if to warn the listeners. I see a famous artist. He works in wood. He stretches his limbs out in a chair and passersby have to navigate around him. He breathes heavily like a beached sea creature. His eyes are red. He is not talking to anybody. I go over to talk to him. He tells me that his gallery owner is cheating him. He tells me that his child is afraid of dogs. He tells me that he was born in Kansas on a farm. I want to know about his farm. He doesn't want to tell me. "Good sunsets?" I ask. "Cow dung," he answers, "great piles of cow dung." "Oh." I change the subject. His head is bald. It has a few red patches along the crown. I wonder if he has a skin disease, psoriasis, impetigo, eczema, poison ivy? His hands are stained orange and his neck is thick. His arms are muscular. His wide fingers run through my hair. Will the stain come off? "Nobody has hair like this in Kansas," he says. I know where he is going. I know why my hair is different from the girls in Kansas. I don't say anything. He closes his eyes and falls asleep in the chair, unless he has passed out. I worry for a moment. Should I tell someone to pay attention to the body in the chair? I don't. Everyone in the room can see him if they wanted to. An hour later I pass by the chair. He is in the same position. I put my hand on his heart. It's beating. He grabs my hand and puts it on his penis. I hope nobody sees this. I pull my hand away. He has not opened his eyes. I leave him alone.

There is my husband over by the bar. He is talking about a flush he pulled in a poker game in the East Village some nights before. His eyes flash, that black flash. Was Dorian Gray this beautiful? I wondered. His long neck turns toward me and he sees me. He seems not to recognize me. I don't go over to him.

He is talking to a writer of a brilliant pornographic book, about to be made into a movie. Perhaps it is not pornography. Perhaps pornography is only a word for prejudice, small-mindedness, limited capacity for joy. I believe that. On the other hand this writer of pornography has droopy eyelids, a smile that seems more of a tic than a smile. He is talking about cunts. He has seen thousands of cunts and prefers women seen from the back. He makes a case for imagination versus reality. I am listening. My husband is fixing himself another drink. I think I don't want the writer of pornography to touch me. He doesn't look like the kind of man who washes his hands often. I move away.

    I am in the arms of a tall blond man. Christopher Worth, III. He is intelligent in a particular way, logical, clear, curious, unconventional while looking like convention itself. He is an old friend of George's maybe from St. Bernard's, maybe from prep school. They shared a whole male world of sports and scores and girls and he smelled of beaches and mothers who worked for the League of Women Voters and sisters who went to dances I wasn't invited to. He was in Paris with George. He was at Harvard with George. He tells me that he would like to feel my breasts. He tells me that he has hitchhiked around Turkey and just returned to write a book on his experiences. Tell me about Turkey, I say. He leads me into the bedroom where my baby is sleeping between a mink and a camouflage jacket. He speaks of Saint Augustine and his genius at self-humiliation. I speak of Saint Benedict, whose thirteen steps I had studied in what seems a distant era. He holds me close. He towers over me. I can feel his heart beating. He takes off his jacket and his tie and throws them on the floor. He is married. So am I. I am afraid of the things that happen in the dark. He is not. We part for the moment. We both know it is just a temporary postponement. "Will you remember my telephone number?" I ask. "Yes," he says. I pick up the baby and put on my coat. My husband will stay for hours more. I will walk down the long street to York Avenue and will wait for a cab to come by. It is late. There are few cabs in the street. Each one already carries a passenger.

In Paris I saw women of the night leaning against the lampposts. In Amsterdam I saw them leaning on their elbows, looking out of windows, wearing nothing but ribbons around their necks. I hold my baby close to me. I am not alone.

John Cheever has taken his scalpel and moved to the suburbs. Those commuters whose wives are driving to ballet classes with their children in the backseats of station wagons, those commuters are daydreaming of escape with a neighbor, of running with the bulls in Pamplona, of killing their fathers, of being under par at Saturday's game. They will do none of these things. They will rot in their places because that is the way it is. It is to escape the rotting that I go to George Plimpton's parties. Artists and writers and their molls don't decay. They explode, perhaps, which is much better. I think of Hemingway and his big fish. A man needs something large to fight, some war perhaps in which evil wears black and good is dressed in khaki. He needs to fight a devil who would oppress, torture, destroy the good people who harvest the wheat and go to church and try to sell their fruit in the market. But no one believes anymore that the devil can be fought. He can leave one place and reappear in another. He exists in the human heart as our favorite lover. Nothing will ever improve. I know that, I have read Dostoevsky. Standing at the corner holding my baby, who woke and cried, wrapped in a Mexican shawl I bought on Eighth Street, I remind myself that I don't like Dostoevsky. I agree with Chekhov, the orchards are gone. A taxi stops. I get in and give the driver my address. The baby wakes again as I close the cab door. She cries all the way home. I try to nurse her but that is not what she wants. She probably wants God and I can't deliver. The night doorman looks at me through bleary eyes. "Keeping the little one out late," he says. She is still crying. "What is wrong, what is wrong," I whisper in her ear.

1953: William Buckley, who had just written *God and Man at Yale*, had two sisters who were Smith alumnae. They sent out a letter to all the college community complaining that two male art teachers who lived together were Communists and should be fired. They asked that no contributions be made to the college until those men were gone. The president of the college, Benjamin Fletcher Wright, stood up at the weekly chapel and announced that he would not be intimidated. He would not fire anyone without evidence of wrongdoing. He was a tall gaunt man. He stood at the podium in front of the large Bible from which he usually read a passage and he spoke of his belief in free speech and then he put his large hands on either side of the open book and he slammed it shut for emphasis, in anger. The sound of the slam echoed through the chapel. I was awed. Someone at the chapel told the Buckley sisters and they began a campaign to get him fired for slamming the Bible. I wrote him a letter of support. But what was I, just a freshman with a throbbing sense of social injustice and a deep inner lake of homesickness for a home that wasn't and could never be, a lake that would flood its banks day after day.

Upon arrival on the campus the Jewish girls were given a sister who was also Jewish and the Catholic girls were given Catholic sisters. My Jewish sister soon left me alone. I wanted to be a part of the whole world. I resented the idea that I would be more comfortable with someone from my tribe. I didn't believe in tribes. I wouldn't join the Hillel house. I wouldn't sit with the other New Yorkers. I wouldn't talk to my best male friend—the boy whose nanny was friends with my nanny—who was at Amherst. I thought he was a fool because he joined a Jewish fraternity. He wrote me a sad letter. I didn't answer it.

Then there was the house kleptomaniac. Someone was breaking into girl's rooms and stealing pins, pearls, cashmere sweaters, Bermuda shorts, scarves, perfumes. Everyone was very upset. Who was the thief? When was it happening? In the small hours of the morning girls in bathrobes patrolled the halls. And then the housemother called me into her rooms to ask me if I was the one. She explained to me that kleptomania was an illness. She said no one would be angry. She would refer me to the school psychiatrist. I wasn't the one. I was the one making statements in support of those accused of Communist sympathies. I was the one who talked about the Negro problem in America, and I was the one who probably looked like an anarchist about to explode. The senior girl, president of the house, asked me to confess, also offering psychiatric counseling. I could feel groups of girls at breakfast tables, at dinnertime, looking at me, staring. They were sure that I was the thief. I wasn't a thief—I was just a seventeen-year-old who wanted to go to Paris and sit at a café with Lady Brett Ashley or Robert Jordan. I was sorry the Spanish civil war was over. There was no Resistance for me to join. I was surely an irritant to all around, nevertheless I had not stolen anything. My good name had been stolen from me.

Then they did a room check and found everyone's property—scarves, pins, wallets—on the top closet shelf of a quiet girl with flat stringy hair from a small Midwest town who was knitting blue-and-white argyle socks for a boyfriend at Yale. No one apologized. I took all the silver from the dining-room drawers and hid it under the couch in the long living room. No one dared ask me if I knew where the silver might be. Four days later I returned the silver to its proper place. But I made plans to escape Northampton.

1960: As the dawn comes up over the Triborough Bridge and the sky shrouds the city in anxious sleep, my husband turns his key in the door. His hair is stringy. His eyes are bloodshot. His jacket is stained. He falls into our bed just as the baby wakes again to begin another day.

They taught us in school that T. S. Eliot's *The Waste Land*

was about the sour taste of human sweat. We were corrupted beyond redemption. There was hope in Eliot's poem, however, because he was able to write it. The artist who interprets the darkness is the redeeming light of humanity, or so it was said. No one claimed that the revolutionary who threw a bomb at the czar or the fellows who wrote the Declaration of Independence or the heroes of the RAF were lights unto humanity. They were mere human clay. It was the artists who transcended, who will remain when all the dross is cleared away. Perhaps this was because all our professors were afraid of being called Communists and fired. Or perhaps it was because Freud had seen into the soul and found it divided into three parts—ego, id, and superego—and even working together, which they never did, these three parts could not cleanse us of our corrupt condition.

If Auden said the lights were going out, he was making the dark into a work of art. If Proust described the Baron de Charlus's exotic tastes, he was making art out of the needs of the body. If Picasso saw the flayed flesh of Guernica, he was making art out of our fury. Language, form was our redemption. It is our best human asset, in place of long teeth and sharp claws. There is a Jewish idea that at the creation of the world the spirit of God, the Shekinah (His female aspect, His soul), was broken as if it were a glass jar dropped, shattered into a million small pieces, and our human job was through good deeds to put the pieces of the jar together again and when we have done so the end of time will come and all will be reconciled between God and His creation. In the universities of America the decade after the war ended, leaving most people eager to build and make and have babies, the professors turned to art as the means to repair the jar, as the way to heal the breach and once again to move toward redemption, but it couldn't be said like that. It had to be expressed in the dark terms of existential eternity, space without end or purpose, man without significance in that space, except for the sentences he could create. Our purpose in life became not to build a high tower, or create a good government, or heal the sick, or end the suffering of the sick; it became to write a poem, a sentence, a novel, a play, or perhaps to do a sculpture or a painting that would serve as witness, witness to the folly of human life.

1963: At George's Chris was waiting for me in the bedroom the following Friday night as I put the baby down. He put his arms around me. He smelled of soap. His skin was pale and even his eyelashes were blond. I had dark hair on my arms, black eyebrows that I had tried to shape but that still sat thick and heavy on my brow. Someone told me that hairy women are fertile. That comforted me because I was a hairy woman. I smelled of baby powder and cream for diaper rash. Chris and I talked about Jean Anouilh. We talked about Ignazio Silone. It didn't matter what we said. We went into the bathroom and Chris locked the door. His hands were between my legs. His drink was placed on the sink. His lit cigarette burned away on the rim of the tub. His wife was in the living room and her babies were home with the nanny and my heart was broken because this wasn't what I really wanted—to be a dark thick-haired girl who was had in someone else's bathroom. On the other hand I didn't want to be a suburban housewife waiting at the train station for a husband who had taken a secretary into the bathroom earlier in the afternoon.

At least I knew that I would grow wise near men who did not follow the stock market, who did not play golf, but who stayed up until the early hours seeing who could be the cleverest most unusual man in the room. This was a competition worth attending. This was a ballet of enormous drama. And I was grateful to be a witness.

Despite the heavy air of flirtation, the perfume of illicit sex that wafted through the book-filled rooms of George's apartment, the game was something else. It was the famous men or the would-be-famous men flexing their skills, strutting their stuff, talking of agents and publishers and rights to this or that. It was the writers impressing each other, hoping to triumph over the one who was talking with an anecdote even more pointed, even more outrageous. It was never about seduction or the women at the edges of the conversation. We girls, not yet called women, were like the Greek chorus, mopping up after the battle was over, emptying ashtrays, carrying the glasses to the sink. The main event was man to man, writer to writer, Mailer to Humes, Plimpton to Matthiessen and even the less well known, the younger, and the stargazers, even they were looking to impress someone with a story, with a witticism, and when that failed with a joke or a major pass-out on the couch. You could feel it in the air, a prep-school dorm, a question of who would win the tennis trophy for the year, a matter of who was the smartest on the debate team, who was the best at wrestling, who could hold their liquor and who could not. I knew enough not to talk too much. It would be fatally wrong in the Plimpton living room, like speaking out your own lines in the theater while the curtain was up and the actors were performing. As the evening wore on the voices grew louder and the lights somehow dimmed and the smell of cigarettes became intense and across the floor a trail of ashes followed in the footsteps of those rising and moving about. The air became stale and the bottles on the bar were nearly empty of liquid and the record player (was it Ella singing?) was gentle, a soft sound in a loud place. Outside the apartment boats on the river slipped by in silence, their lights blinking against the dark steel shapes of the nearby bridge.

And of course I did love Chris, a forbidden wisp of a love, not disagreeable at all.

1957–1965: After a while Wolf tired of his haphazard family or perhaps he was simply infected by the American dream of moving on and up. He left for California with a model who was a client and was never heard from again. And I introduced Nora to a designer of toys who was the son of a friend of my mother. Immediately they fell in love and they had babies. Nora believed in having babies at home, no hospital, no forceps, just music and a midwife and her own pillows and the other children gathered around. I was a little worried about that. What

about cords around the neck? What about upside-down babies? What about hemorrhages? Nora believed that natural childbirth would be fine and it was. She had four little boys in a row. She had six children now.

But she was not completely happy and so she went into therapy with a psychologist who had his office in her apartment building. The psychologist was married and lived in New Jersey just across the bridge. Taboos are there for the breaking and the strong convictions by most professionals that doctors should not sleep with their patients was soon ignored by this therapeutic couple. Nora said it was natural that she should love this wonderful doctor. He left his wife and children and moved into her apartment and the toy designer moved out. Yes, it is possible to love and love again and each time to pack your suitcase, change your address, and bring your children along on an adventure in self-discovery.

And then they moved to New Jersey and the key parties were beginning and one night Nora brought home a different husband and father and this one wanted to stay with her and so he did. The psychiatrist left. I never went to a key party because I never went to a party where people needed to drive in order to arrive and go home. I accepted the forward-looking view of those who supported open marriage and I preferred all things on the table to the hypocrisy I had known as a child but I had an unspoken reservation: Are the children all right? And is it possible that one can love a single person all life through and never betray them, never need another body, wait at night for the bed to warm in the old familiar way? I knew the idea was old-fashioned like my mother's dozens of white gloves piled up in a slender drawer.

1962: Jack and I rent a house in East Hampton for the summer. That is to say my mother rents this house for us. It is small and down an alley but I am happy to be near the beach. Jack complains that my mother should have rented a bigger house. We meet the Reasons. He is a man with one brown eye and one blue eye. He is a lyricist. He has written the words to a song that Elvis Presley has made as common as salt on the dinner table. He had dropped out of high school and gone to LA and gotten a job at a music building as a messenger boy and when the elevator stopped on a particular floor he heard Negro music and he had the novel idea of getting a white man to sing like that. And by the time he was nineteen he had enough money to live like a pasha for the rest of his life. He would never have to work again. He has a wife, Tessa, who is an actress, a woman who had arrived in America as a refugee from Germany. She had lived a while in Cuba. She knew how close she came to extinction. She was a nervous but lovely bird, a fragile tremble about her, a dash of fear in her eyes, a feminine way of crossing and uncrossing her legs, the manner of a waif or a coquette or both, and she had beautiful freckles on her arms, and she knew all sorts of actors because her father was an important theater director. She had no exact accent and yet there was something in her inflection, something throaty and wild that made you know she came from somewhere else.

The Reasons had big parties in the mansion they had rented on Ocean Avenue and they hung lanterns along the porch columns and they had musicians play and waiters brought drinks on silver trays and the guests went barefoot on the grass or sat on the floor inside and told stories. The fireflies flew about the night lawn and the women wore blouses with embroidery made in far-off countries and sandals and the smell of pot floated out from under the trees and my baby slept in the upstairs bedroom with the Reasons' two boys, watched over by the nanny who never went home.

Tessa wanted to produce and star in a play. Several painters and playwrights had ideas for an abstract event. We talked about doing another happening. The Reasons were willing to lend their lawn for a happening. What was to happen? The answer was vague — music, color, dance, a mood evoked, a chill confronted. It was to be strange and otherworldly. It was to make us feel unreal. But we already felt unreal. The Reasons shouted at each other under the maple tree. In other summers the rented house had seen more decorous tenants.

I sit on a chair and next to a cartoonist. He is Australian. He brings me a drink. I spill it on the grass and he offers to get me another. I have seen his illustrations in the bookstore. I tell him that I admire his work. I do. He offers to give me an original illustration. Come with me now, he says, and you can pick the one you want. Yes, I say. We drive off in his car. His wife has her arm around a poet who is much younger than she. She doesn't notice us get into their car. We arrive at his house and the lights are on. His little daughter is asleep in her bedroom. The nanny is in the kitchen. Drawings of his are on the living-room walls. Everything is white and clean, no chintz, no antiques, no smell of other times, just the whiteness of the walls that makes you think of sheets, bedroom sheets. He takes me up to the attic where his studio is and opens for me a long cardboard box in which rests a Barbie doll, a small Barbie doll. "I have made for her," he says, "some clothes." And as he lifts her out of her box I see that she is wearing a tiny black leather belt and there is a little metal chain around her wrist and she has dark stockings pulled up to her vagina, which has been painted red. She wears a bracelet decorated with nails sticking out. There is a tiny guillotine and a Barbie stands behind it holding a black whip. Another Barbie is pouring something out of a pitcher into the mouth of a tiny dragon. It is red and plastic. I look at the display. I will not be shocked. I have read the Marquis de Sade. "This is amazing," I say. "You like it?" he says. "I do," I say. What else do you say to an artist? I notice the Barbie with blood pouring out of her nipples and an ax, a little miniature ax stuck in her scalp. The doll's blond hair is still in place with a small perfect flip at the ends. One of her eyes has been gouged out and the eye rests on her cheek. There is a cot in the studio. There are some drawings of alligators and elephants on the walls. He offers me a cigarette. He puts his hand on my neck. He is very big and strong. I think for a second he might break my neck, the bone would snap and the baby would have no mother. But he just lets his fingers lie there. I do not bend toward him. I should put my hand there or there. I don't. I am afraid. I am afraid of his Barbies.

I want to go back to the party. The illustrator gives me an illustration of a man with a bare ass being whipped by a naked girl in fox furs. "Look," he says and he shows me some hidden fornicating bodies in the design on the first page of his book on wildlife in Africa. I would never have seen them on my own. He wants to take me into the bedroom. I run to the front door. "I'll drive you back," he says. And he does. And we don't talk anymore. The truth is I am afraid of him. I am also ashamed of being afraid of him. I want to experience all that is human. I do, but not just yet.

No one has noticed my absence. I go upstairs, the baby is sleeping. I have no love but my love for the baby. I join the party. Down the road the ocean waited. I wanted to sit on the night beach and watch the glowworms light up the sand, millimeter by millimeter. My husband was telling a story about a mathematician who had killed himself because he had solved the proof he had been working on for forty years. He had no interest in coming with me to the beach. I walked to the parking lot, dark except for the light on the bathhouse deck. I sat on a bench and breathed in the salt air. I wanted to lie down with my baby in a bed and go to sleep. As I walked back toward the party I heard the lyrics "You ain't nothing but a hound dog, Cryin' all the time," the music rising and falling, the beat strong, the bass loud, the melody in my brain was slower, more a light rainfall on the roof in the spring.

In my dream later that night I saw amber urine flow over the lawn. In my dream the night sky turned amber. I saw the water from the tap in the kitchen flow amber. This was the color of

ease, of forgetting, of parties, of strangers, of words that didn't
need to make sense. This was the color of scotch and bourbon
and ambition soaked in fear, and as I tried to find shelter under
a tree from the amber sky the rain came down and each drop
called out failure . . . you and you and you . . . failures all.

Failure because the expectations were so high. For Jack it
remained Keats coughing out his young heart that he had to
surpass by a certain day. For others it was their own idols . . .
men of such gifts that one hundred, two hundred years later
their names were known to everyone who could read or went to
a museum. Immortality, that was what they wanted. Recognition
for their unique minds, for their unique way with stone or words
or paint. It wasn't enough for their mothers or their girlfriends or
their wives to applaud their efforts. They were after immortality:
the fool's gold that waits under the imaginary rainbow. And
under the lanterns on the Reasons' lawn, scattered beneath the
columns of the sedate mansion that should never have been
rented to the likes of these, a mansion that had seen bankers and
stockbrokers, families with names on boxes at the opera, families
who belonged in this mansion, drank the artists, playwrights,
novelists, poets. At the Moulin Rouge the misshapen body of
Toulouse-Lautrec waited out the long hours until dawn,
postponing the moment when the morning light would leave
him once again in his bed alone, still a cripple. No one on the
Reasons' lawn was dwarfed of limb but almost all of us carried
an inner hump.

No one was humpier than the painter who earlier that
evening had injected himself with heroin behind the spreading

oak. His blue eyes were wide and his drink had spilled on his multicolored shirt and there was a vein in his ankle that seemed to have blown up like a tiny balloon. He played the clarinet and his instrument sat by his side like a pet lizard waiting to be fed. The night had turned cold and the wind from the sea caused the lanterns to rustle and rattle and a woman who wore no underwear beneath her miniskirt sat on the front steps, her legs spread wide apart, mewing or crying and calling for the man she had arrived with who was nowhere to be found. Tessa sent a waiter to look for him in the gazebo at the back of the house. I sat next to the woman and put my arms around her to make her stop crying. She stopped. When I stood up she pulled at my skirt, tearing a rip with her nails. The sculptor who made large wood shapes reminiscent of bears but not quite and put them all over his lawn pulled me onto a porch swing. I thought he smelled of bear but perhaps it was only his leather vest with the Indian-like beads on strings that hung from the shoulders.

Excuse me, I said, I need to go find my husband. But my husband was in the middle of a circle of men, they were talking about Camus's death: Suicide or accident? A great literary misfortune for the world or a fitting end to a life of moving too close to the flame? He was speeding. He had no will to live. He was a great writer. Not as great as Baudelaire. Not a poet. Just a corpse. The men were shouting. Something was at stake. What was it? He died like Jackson someone said. Jackson Pollock had smashed his car into a tree after a night of partying, taking a woman with him. And there was silence in the group. Awe perhaps. Those who thought they could avoid disaster felt superior to Jackson spread apart into pieces on the road. Those who sought death were jealous of Jackson, his oils, his enzymes, his brain cells, his hemoglobin sinking into the tar. "He took two women with him," I say. But no one heard me.

The celebrated young playwright Jack Gelber is at the party with his wife, Carol. He has written a play about drugs that is the talk of off Broadway. He has a sweet face. He wears jeans and a polo shirt. He is not a druggie himself. But he knows about it. How does he know about it? He is the father of a boy and a girl just a little older than my baby. His wife wears a smile on her face like other women wear their pearls. She is happy to be at the party. I want to be happy to be at this party. Tessa comes toward me, her full breasts, her small hips, the tears that wet the lashes but do not fall, the refugee look in her eyes, the waif that has no home comes and holds my hand. I am grateful. Tessa gets up to dance. I watch her. And then I fall asleep in the porch chair.

1956: My roommate at Sarah Lawrence is sleeping with her boyfriend who is at Princeton. The problem is that he doesn't stay in Princeton—very often he spent the night in our bathtub because our beds are too narrow for two bodies. I wake in the morning and see his long arms dangling out the side of the bathtub. His name is Rufus. He writes poetry. Everyone writes poetry. Everyone at Sarah Lawrence knows that the black-haired girl with a fierce glare is sleeping with our art history professor. He picks her up in his car and takes her to his

Manhattan penthouse every weekend. I meet her at a bar on MacDougal Street. She is sitting alone at a table. She offers me a cigarette. She tells me that she is through with him. He is too old. He bores her. A man comes in and joins us. He says he has a gun. He talks about Cuba. In America, he says, everyone should have a gun. I leave.

Everyone knows that the tall broad girl with the dusty-blond hair that hangs in oily strings about her face is having an affair with another girl on her dormitory floor. The two of them sit in the dining room and no one else approaches their table. The blonde wears a chain around her waist. She has a boy's leather jacket and the other one has cut her hair almost to her scalp. This is very interesting. I would like to talk to them but I'm not sure how to approach them.

I finally sit down at their table and I tell them that I believe that Emily Dickinson is gay. We establish that I am not—not yet, one says. They invite me to a bar in the Village, all women.

It is dark in the bar. I can hardly make out the faces of the women who crowd the barstools, who lean against the wall, who sit in groups of four and five at the tables. I think some of them are men. They are not. My Sarah Lawrence friends disappear in the back of the bar. I am alone, eating the cherry in my whiskey sour. I don't like the taste of the drink. I am not alone for long. A woman with very wide thighs and wearing a motorcycle jacket asks me to join her table, a woman with a pretty blouse all covered in sequins asks me to go outside with her for a quiet talk. I see blazers, jodhpurs, black boots. I see ballet shoes. I see women with lipstick dark as wine and rouge applied as if for a clown's role. I see women with small mustaches painted on and women decorated with only the natural pallor of the skin, the way men walk around, undisguised. I see women with the backs of their necks shaved clean and women wearing thick black belts with gold buckles. There is a whole world here that would welcome me if I choose to join it. My heart pounds. I am alarmed. Have I entered an underground from which I will never exit? An older woman comes over and tells me that I have a darling face. Do I have a darling face? I am pleased but worried, do I want her to think I have a darling face?

There are fedoras hung on pegs near the door. There are fat dykes and skinny ones along the bar. They call themselves dykes. I think perhaps that's a rude word but maybe I'm wrong. Everything isn't in a box. Women can look like men and wear men's clothes and sex can be free of pregnancy and marriage, and touch and smell, body to body, need not be the way it is in the movies. I tell myself that. Still before the night is over I know I'm never coming back. In part because I am a coward and in part because I am not on fire. I am curious but cautious. The bar feels like the anteroom to Hades, the boathouse where one waits to cross the river Styx. I am not ready. I want babies. I am, despite my black leotard, my blue beret, my tight jeans, unwilling to go home with any of the women in the bar. My eyes are stinging from the clouds of smoke. I cough every now and then.

Soon there are rumors around that my two friends are being thrown out of Sarah Lawrence for lesbian activities. One leaves, the other does not. Perhaps they weren't thrown out of school.

Perhaps they had a fight and parted ways and one wanted to go somewhere else without a reminder of her lost love.

I read Radclyffe Hall's *The Well of Loneliness*. I paid rapt attention to the outlaw acts in the book and the sadness of the narrator. Someone told me that Swann's love of Odette was really about Proust's love for a man. But over the subject hung the curtains of secrecy, the sense of transgression, of vileness, of perversion, of shame.

My uncle, alarmed at my costume of jeans and a black T-shirt, asked me if I liked boys. He said that a woman's role was to get married and have children and if I didn't do that I would be an outcast and a disgrace to the family.

There was a very beautiful lesbian who hung out in Paris and dressed like a man. Her name was Natalie Barney and she knew all the great writers and she had a big table in one of the major cafés in Paris and she always wore evening dress, a man's tie and a black hat. She carried a long black cigarette holder. She was surrounded by women in low-cut gowns. She was as brilliant as she was beautiful, it was said. She was never found in the market buying bananas. She wasn't spending afternoons in the Tuileries watching children chasing balls. She was a butterfly of the night, a falcon unafraid of the dark. She was like the unicorn in the tapestry in the cloister: likely imaginary. I read Djuna Barnes, *Nightwood*. I understood not a word. But she was a lesbian who was a friend of T. S. Eliot. In the miles and miles of suburbs that spread out from the city, in the car washes and the supermarkets and the golf clubs no one knew her name. They didn't know T. S. Eliot, either. As far as I was concerned they didn't know anything worth knowing at all. I didn't think Milton Berle was funny. I didn't watch *The Ed Sullivan Show*. I thought there was a tumor in America's brain and it would spread until all that remained was the limbic tissues that made us kin to alligators.

1962: There is a happening in the woods, an heiress from Texas owns the woods. We go with blankets and flashlights. The cars park on the side of the road and we walk on a path to a clearing. There are blue strobe lights circling the center of the area. There are strange sounds from wood instruments. There is a white flag that is raised and lowered over and over again on a high pole. There are bird sounds and gunshots and a tank made of cardboard rides around, or perhaps it was an airplane or an abstract object. There is a strange smell, sulfur perhaps. There is a coffin carried by four dancers in black leotards. The coffin is opened and a man in a clown mask jumps out and runs away. More music. More lights. Something has happened. What has happened? Scotch and bourbon and beer has happened and bottles lie about everywhere. Someone is sleeping in someone's lap. Someone is having sex behind the trees. Are the moans part of the happening or not? It is time, I think, to stop trying to make sense of anything. That is the message of the happening. My soon-to-be ex-husband has wandered off. My baby is afraid of the noise and the crowd that is now pushing toward their cars. Felicity, a woman I had met at the Reasons' party a few nights before, offers to hold my blanket for me. Her husband is Lewis and they have just bought a large old house right before the turn toward Main Street. He is still in his twenties as are we all. I see him lying on the grass talking to a movie producer who claims he is a porno king. Lewis is a stockbroker, a financial guy, who has made a fortune. That is obvious. He is broad-chested and big, his eyes are cautious. His features flat. He has begun to go bald. His walk is confident, a stride that seems to say: I own the grass I am stepping on, even if I am on someone else's property. The way he holds his head speaks of the high-school football star, the owner of the best car dealership in town. He also is a writer whose novel set on a Sioux reservation is soon to be published by Viking Press. He tells me that he is one-quarter Indian. His grandfather a full-breed Indian.

He and Felicity invite us to a party at their house. There is a bar on the lawn. There are waiters serving drinks. The Gelbers are there and a young playwright named Arthur Kopit, who has had a huge success with a play that was first produced when he was an undergraduate at Harvard. Lewis is a talker and he moves among his guests like a man who always knew that he would give big parties on the wide lawns of summer houses in the best section of town. The talk is of Cavafy and Lawrence Durrell and on the wide porch Larry Rivers is talking baseball with Willem de Kooning and a man in overalls who has a hammer hanging from his belt. Felicity and I sit on a step near the kitchen door. Her dad has died and her mother is a widow living in Kansas City. Felicity says she is now where she wanted to be all her life. She has long hair that hangs limp around her face, which is marked by the ravages of acne. Her eyes are friendly and kind.

Fortune has been good to her. I am glad. There are fireflies on the lawn and stars in the sky. I have left the baby with a sitter although the baby let out an endless series of earth-shattering sobs when I approached the door and I almost stayed home. I talk to Felicity about Samuel Beckett. She prefers Jean Genet.

And after the party or perhaps it was before the party Lewis gave Jack Gelber a Rolls-Royce. He said he had two and was happy to have one to give his friend. After the party Lewis gave Arthur Kopit a sailboat. And then he gave Jack Gelber a life insurance policy for his family or so it was rumored. He was an extraordinarily generous man and genial man. We picnicked on the beach together. We went to dinner at little restaurants along the highway. We looked at the moon over the ocean together, staying on the beach, smoking, drinking scotch out of thermos bottles.

1966: I have met a doctor who comes to my house for dinner after his last patient. He is courting me. I am willing him to continue. Hope makes me smile in the dark even after he has gone home for the night. Late one evening Lewis called me on the phone.

"I am here in Malibu talking with Marlon Brando," he said, "and we are forming an oil company to do business with Indonesia, an opening market, and I can let you in for $25,000. Your investment will guarantee you $1,000 a month." "Marlon Brando, the real Marlon Brando?" I shout into the phone. "Yes," he says. "Are you in?" My mother had died a few years earlier and left me a $25,000 life insurance policy. "No," said the man in my bed, "that money should stay in your account in the bank." "No," I said to Lewis, "I can't, but thank you for thinking of me." The first week of the next month I receive a check for $1,000 from a company with an Indonesian address. "Look," I say to the man who will become my husband. "We could have made $1,000." I call Lewis. He tells me the check was issued by accident when he thought I would be in with the others who had joined the oil company. I put the check in an envelope and mailed it back. The next month another check came. I returned it. And the month after that another and then they stopped.

SUMMER OUT ON the main beach at East Hampton, where we gathered on the left side of the lifeguard stand as usual. The Gelber children, Niles Southern, my daughter played by the edge of the ocean while we sat under umbrellas. Behind us a painter from Paris had set up his beach tent which had long flowing white panels. He lay on a chair surrounded by three women in bikini bottoms and no tops. Their thin bodies glistened with oil. Their long hair floated in the breezes that blew off the sea. The painter was famous. His picnic basket was filled with pâté and *fromages* with mysterious names. If the wind came from the north we smelled something illegal, something sweet and promising coming from inside the tent. The tent kept the sun at bay and the curious eyes of strangers could catch no more than a quick glimpse of a perfect bowl of fruit resting on a white box. At the afternoon's end the tent was folded quickly and several men carried the provisions off to a waiting car. The artist disappeared in a puff of activity.

Lewis went into the ocean and stood about chest-deep and began to punch at the oncoming waves. He hit one after another with all his strength and still they kept coming, as waves will. They splashed over him and pushed against his wide chest and he would emerge and punch again and again. Was he pretending to be King Canute? Did he know we were all watching? Felicity tried to get him out of the water but he shouted at her to leave him alone. It went on for hours. Day after day as we drank iced tea and the smell of oil and egg-salad sandwiches rose around us, as the children dripped ice cream on their sandy skin we watched. As the sun faded the thermoses appeared with gin and vodka and someone brought lemon slices and the gulls picked at the afternoon's droppings and the terns scurried in the ocean's foam and finally Lewis would emerge from the water and lie down on a towel and fall asleep as the rest of us packed up to go home.

Early in the fall I was having a dinner party. My husband-to-be had come over with several bottles of wine. Just five couples, among them Felicity and Lewis were expected. The party was called for eight so I could get the child to sleep. The phone rang. It was Felicity. She was so sorry but they would have to cancel, at such short notice, Lewis had been arrested. The police had showed up at the door and taken him off just as he was dressing for dinner.

What had happened? We gradually pieced the story

together. Lewis had been a door-to-door magazine salesman when he and Nora had moved to an apartment on Varick Street. Lewis had wanted to live in the heart of the Village with the artists and writers. The corner grocer on Varick Street was an older man ready to sell his store and retire to his home in the Bronx. He told Lewis about his plans when Lewis stopped in to buy some beer on his way home. Lewis told him he was a stockbroker and could invest his money for him with his brokerage firm. This would guarantee the grocer $1,000 a month income for the rest of his life. And so it began. There was of course no brokerage firm only a package of forms for subscriptions to *The Saturday Evening Post, Pageant, Look,* and *Life*.

Lewis then took the grocer's life savings and bought the house in East Hampton and the boat and the cars and the friendship of the crowd he ran with. The parties were paid for with the profits that came from a pound of tomatoes and a can of peaches. He did send the grocer $1,000 a month as long as he could. He also took his mother-in-law's life savings and promised to invest them well and she too received $1,000 a month until the money was all gone. A few of the people who came to the parties invested in the oil deal and others gave him money as a stockbroker. And one day it was all gone and there was nothing to give anyone and the grocer who had not received his check for months complained to the police and it was over just like that. Lewis was sentenced to the psychiatric ward at Columbia-Presbyterian where he stayed about three weeks and then one morning they found his bed empty, his small suitcase gone. He had fled with another patient, a woman, and disappeared out West where someone said he was selling real estate to retirees.

Viking was not publishing his novel. One of our friends was an editor at Viking. He had been at many dinners with Lewis. He was told that Lewis's novel was being published by his house. He did not say anything to us about the possibility that this was not true. His first thought, he later admitted, was that he was being cut out by someone else in his office who was keeping the full list from him. He didn't want to admit to anyone that he was being excluded so he said nothing until it turned out that there was no book on the Sioux and there was no contract and it was all a fiction. No, it wasn't a fiction. It was a swindle, it was a lie, it was a crime. The question for all of us was how did we not know? How could a man take a Rolls-Royce or a boat from a man and not know the mind of his benefactor: not see that it was all a way to buy a place in a world that was itself just one of the many shadows on the cave's walls? Were we all characters in a second-rate summer-stock play?

No man can defeat the ocean.

And what of the grocer? He is after all the central character in this tale. Perhaps English wasn't his first language. He had worked how many days, years, hours behind his counter to save this money? How was he to live now that it was gone? Did he die soon after? Did he leave a widow to sit on the benches on the Grand Concourse holding a battered leather purse, in it the half a sandwich she was saving for dinner? I don't know what the Gelbers did with the Rolls-Royce. Did they actually receive it or was that just talk. I don't know how long the boat that Arthur

Kopit sailed in the bay lasted or even if it really existed. I do
know that fame and fortune, name-in-the-paper fame, money-in-
the-bank fortune, big-house-in-the-Hamptons fortune, or more
important recognition fortune, *ah there he is, the man in the
corner with the red suspenders, there he is the man on the beach
in the striped bathing suit, the man with the beer in his hand, the
man sleeping under the oak on someone else's lawn, the writer, the
painter, the sculptor, the moviemaker, the genius, the man at
Elaine's when it closes, the last one out the door, weaving his way
down the street, that man, the famous man, that passion for
success, served like blinders, so that no one could see a fraud when
a fraud was visible, right there in front of your very eyes.* Perhaps
none of us saw the other, knew the other, like the shades in
Hades, we wandered around, the fog too heavy, the light too
dim.

1962: And so Jack's play was going to open on Broadway.
It was being directed by Arthur Penn, a director with a fine
reputation and a keen mind. He had directed Anne Bancroft in
The Miracle Worker and was a man to stare at when he walked
through a room. The play starred Alfred Drake, who had played
the lead in many musicals. This was to be his first straight acting
role. The play was about a troupe of actors in Italy wandering
from town to town. The plot has faded in my mind. I thought it
was brilliant. I thought the play as fine as anything Shaw had
ever written. I thought it would earn my husband the place in
the firmament that he sought, and then perhaps he would stop

wandering and drinking and shaking his arms in front of his face for hours at a time, and then perhaps he would see that he loved me and our child, and then perhaps, sated by fame, he could find with me whatever he sought in the predawn hours with women of the street.

The *Daily News* takes a photo of me with the child on my lap. I am wearing a black silk dress with a gold circle pin and the child is raising her arms in excitement at something she sees across the room. There is a photo in *Vogue* of the new playwrights, Jack and Jack Gelber, Arthur Kopit and Edward Albee. I think they are standing on boxes or in boxes but perhaps that is a false memory. The theater will be saved by these young men. The always dying theater has been reprieved. We are invited to Irene Selznick's home for dinner. We are invited to her house in the country. We are invited to Lee Strasberg's party. He is the famous acting teacher, the Actors Studio has produced Marlon Brando. Strasberg's own daughter has played Anne Frank. Here the actors learn to search their own souls for the emotions that float beneath the character's lines. Here Freud casts his shadow. In the depth of the soul lies universal truth. If you need tears think on a sad event in your own story. Every actor has a sad story or they wouldn't be standing on a stage asking us to look at them, listen to them. They would wear their own faces and go about their business like the people who sell car insurance or the housewives who make fruit Jell-O.

Everyone is at the Strasbergs' party. The stars and would-be stars, the producers and directors and their wives. It is as if there is a center to the theater world and a permanent party goes on at this center and if you are there you are forever eating canapés and sitting on sofas in grand apartments that look out over the park. And people are kissing you and the volume of the voices is turned up as high as it can go and the shy ones wear skimpy dresses and totter on high heels and look ready to cry if a director should ask them, or even if he doesn't. The directors are male. The producers are male. The agents are mostly male. The agent who has taken Jack on is an older man who knows everyone. It is about knowing everyone. The agent, Harold Friedman, admires Jack. He is a short round man with kind eyes who wants Jack to meet a famous set designer, an important publicist, a theater owner. I am left on my own. I find an actor who has appeared in the chorus of *South Pacific*. He tells me the story of his flight from Omaha and his arrival on Broadway and his plans to play Richard the Third in summer stock. He likes Jews, he tells me. They are passionate in bed. Are we, I wonder? How does he know? He will invite me for a drink after the party. I have to go home to the child. I want to go home to the child. At these parties I often perspire heavily. Sometimes I can smell myself, a dank strange odor like that of a small animal in a cage. No product saves me. Perhaps I was meant to live on a farm. I am always worried that dark circles will appear under my arms. I keep my arms close to my sides.

My friend Tessa, who was an actress, helps me dress and fixes my hair. Tessa shows me how to put makeup on my eyes. But the makeup tends to run down my cheeks. I rub my eyes when I forget that I have lashes brushed with black ink. I fidget while she paints my face. I am not an actress. A mask does not make me more comfortable. I wish I really smoked and didn't just pretend to inhale. Jack's agent has a kind plump motherly wife. Mrs. Friedman tells me that I am lucky to have married such a talented man. She points out the actors to me. This one is in the play at the Majestic. This one is a comic, and that one sings at the Carlyle.

Tessa says I should cut my hair. A comedian named Zero Mostel shows me how he can swallow lit cigarettes. In the park the lights come on. The police are riding down the avenue on horses. I see my husband out of the corner of my eye. He is holding a drink in one hand and his accent, which has a flavor of Eton, is growing stronger. He is talking about Spinoza to a director who does avant-garde plays in small theaters in the West Village. The director says that when he travels he takes a copy of Spinoza in his briefcase. Over there by the couch is the woman rumored to be Jack Kennedy's girlfriend. Someone whispers in my ear that Kennedy comes into the city just to see her. She is a long-legged glorious actress. She has a mane of golden curls that reach halfway down her back. She towers over me. But she is probably just the right size for the president. I have forgotten the name of my second-grade teacher, I have forgotten the name of my professor of ancient history, I have forgotten the name of the doctor who delivered the child, but I remember this actress's name. Was it envy or awe that seared it into my brain?

Perhaps the Strasberg apartment is just a stage set. It will rotate on some invisible axis and the scene will change and will turn into a long line of shabbily dressed people waiting for food at a local church. Jack is talking to Julian Beck who runs an experimental theater group. Mrs. Freidman (time has erased her first name from my brain cells) tells me that her husband's partner has a wife who is also a partner in the agency. This woman, a large-boned, athletic-looking sort with a long beautiful face is having an affair with one of their clients, John P. Marquand. For a moment I wish it were me having an affair with John P. Marquand. He is a writer I too have loved, of course only at a distance, only through his pages. John P. Marquand was much older than I was. He was also an Anglo-Saxon who would not understand the sale of dry goods from a pushcart that brought my grandfather such good fortune. He would not understand the panting hurry of my heart, or the sweating of my rude glands. Or so I think. I also think we have come to the end of the leprechaun's rainbow where fame waits in a pot of gold and fame will save Jack's life. He needs it the way a bird needs the air, to float in, to ride the wind, to last out the storm, to serve its purpose in the scheme of things. I go home, leaving Jack at the party. As the door closes behind me I get a glimpse of him leaning over a woman in a silver sequined top, her blond hair held in place with a black satin headband. She is laughing at something he has said. Something clever I'm sure.

1966: We are in the Hamptons. Niles Southern's daddy has appeared. He has brought Niles a toy car. It is a toy just right for a boy about four years old. But it has a real motor. You can make this car go fast. You need to steer it or it will go into a tree.

It is a red convertible with a real dashboard. It has a brake and a gas pedal. The boys gather around it. Niles is triumphant in his toy. He doesn't want to share it. His mother is smiling her gracious smile. I am an anxious Jewish mother. No, I tell my child, you may not drive it. She screams at me. Other children are fighting and fussing and a brother pulls a sister's shorts down and she weeps. We are gathered around the car in the driveway. Jed Gelber has a fierce light in his eyes. He too is only four or perhaps five. Niles takes the car out of the driveway and along the road. It goes maybe two miles an hour but it goes. A seagull flies above the garbage pail, which sits beside the garage.

Another child is weeping. The jealousy among the children is salty, you can taste it on your tongue. Terry Southern is drinking gin out of a paper cup. He is talking about a deal he has just made in Hollywood, a movie deal, his book will be made into a movie. "So you sold out," says a poet. We laugh as if it were meant as a joke. It isn't a joke. The desire for money is like the deep thirst of a man in a lifeboat lost at sea. He knows that somewhere on the shore other people are drinking freely, carelessly, while he stares at the waves around him and his throat cracks and his heart begins to curl up and his eyes dim. Hollywood is not going to offer our poet a cool drink. The other writers joke: "So, Terry, did you get a starlet with your contract?" Terry nods. He has a pouch in his pocket with something in it. Something he doesn't talk about but is valuable. He disappears around the corner and comes back a while later, his face blotchy and his cigarette burning down dangerously near his lips.

"Give Jed a turn," urges Carol Southern. Niles is a gentle

child with big eyes and a face that has not lost its wonder. He gets up out of his prize car and Jed gets in. Jed presses down on the gas and the car zooms out of the driveway. "Slower," yells his mother. "Careful," says someone. But Jed takes the car at top speed down the road and steers it right into a tree. There is the sound of crunching metal. There is the sound of Jed's howl. We all run down the street. There is Jed, dirt on his face, a scratch on his arm, and there is the prize car, a crumpled, destroyed piece of metal, a little whining sound coming from under the miniature hood. The car is no more. Niles holds his mother's hand. It's all right Niley, she says. It's just a toy. Jed is grinning. A strange demonic grin. He is only a child, a child who didn't want another one to have a marvelous present. My child is clinging to my legs. "It's nothing," says Terry. "I can buy you another one," he says to his child. His wife glares at him. "This is not a toy for a child." By now we can see the sliver of a moon rising above and the air is getting cold. Niles has not said anything. He seems smaller, thinner than an hour ago. Someone jokes about Jed being a junior Jackson, that Jackson Pollock who has killed himself in a car crash on Springs-Fireplace Road some years before. All the men are thinking about agents and advances and movie contracts and the women are worrying about cars going too fast, and trees appearing suddenly in the view, and death, which can only be kept at bay by fame, makes itself known to those of us who stop at lights, signal when turning, and never drive while under the influence.

Also we know not to fall asleep on the beach on Fire Island. The poet Frank O'Hara, at the moment of his ascending reputation, at the moment of his finding his place in the firmament, drank too much and fell asleep on the night beach and a dune buggy rode over him and killed him, right then, when he was dreaming, of what we will never know. Tessa knew him. I did not. She mourned for him. If the modern world still made myths, O'Hara would be a constellation, one that appeared in the summer sky, one that you could see if you laid on your back listening to the July surf slap at the shore. Of course romantic poets are destined to die young. It is part of their appeal. The untimely death, the taking of substances that perhaps damage the brain cells: Coleridge and his opium, "In Xanadu did Kubla Khan a stately pleasure-dome decree . . ." I wonder why cabinetmakers and bankers and insurance men and cobblers and cleaners and doctors and lawyers do not as a rule seek early death. While poets and writers seem so often to find their way to permanent collapse, some death they had been expecting all along. Why did Frank O'Hara lie down in the sand?

It had to do with drink. This was not a charming end. It was not poetic justice. It was a grubby, skin-splitting-in-the-sand, alcohol-pooling-around-crushed-organs death, where flies and sandworms and birds must have pecked at the open wounds before dawn arrived. A sober man would have gone home to bed. A drunk man lay down on the beach in the dark. Drink and writers, writers and drink . . . I thought it as natural as bees and honey, as breasts and milk, as love and pain. That's what happens when common sense is banished from the brain and myth, the Hemingway myth, moves in, preening around, lording it over other thoughts, ruling the brain like some tin-pot dictator of a banana republic.

Jed Gelber had only downed a paper cup half full of fruit punch before he took the wheel of Niles's car. But he was five, or almost five, years old.

Late 1962–1963: The play went into rehearsal. Jack awoke before noon and dressed carefully and went down to the theater to watch and rewrite and in the evening we sometimes went out to dinner with Arthur Penn and his tall beautiful wife. They had two children. They had a house in Massachusetts. They knew everyone in the theater and still a sanity seemed to surround them the way clouds protect the Greek gods until they wish to make themselves visible. Perhaps this was not true. Perhaps they screamed at each other in their bedroom. Perhaps their children had nightmares and failed in school. Perhaps they each loved another who was out of reach. Perhaps they lost the friendship that had once tied them so close. But all I saw was the grace of it. And here was the director who would save Jack's life, bring us together, let us live the way they lived.

As they rehearsed my mother lay in her bed, a brain tumor having made her mute, and I sat by her side, stunned at such a thing as death riding up the elevator with me, following me into her bedroom, biding its time in the closet filled with her party dresses and her fur coat and the wigs that were in fashion that year and the shoes lined up on the shelves with their Cuban heels and little velvet straps and the pocketbooks on a higher shelf, alligator, velvet, gold clasps, silver clasps. Death was in the bathroom and sat on the chair with me and hung almost visible on the dressing table with its white tulle skirt and now its bottles of medicine, useless medicine sitting on the shelf beneath the mirror, replacing the creams and lotions, the gold-cased lipsticks, the powders in their round jars, the perfume in its fluted bottle.

And Alfred Drake, who had never starred in a straight play before, a singer with a deep and stirring baritone, had trouble memorizing his lines and the lead actress was slapped on the face by her boyfriend and had a disfiguring bruise across one cheek and a black eye. A piece of the scenery fell down. There was an air of crisis around the production. There is always an air of crisis in the theater, everyone assured me. Pearl Harbor is always one day away. Disaster threatens. It's good for the show. It keeps everyone on edge, nerves taut, the way they should be. I worry. I can see that Jack's hands are flapping in the closet more often than usual. I can see that he arrives home closer and closer to dawn. After the opening everything will get better, I believe, everything except my mother, a fact I know, the way I know my eyes see the day ahead of me, the rain on the pavement, the umbrella in my hand, the child's tangled hair, but a fact that lies outside my perimeter, a beast I won't see if I don't look, a beast that stays outside and circles the village, biding its time.

The final days of rehearsal arrive. I come one night. Jack is drinking in a bar down the block. I watch the play. I hear its

words. I see the actors. This is the play that I have typed and sent
to Jack's agent to give to a producer. The play that the agent said
was brilliant, that the director admired, that Alfred Drake
wanted to do. I hear a place or two in the first act that could
move faster. I hear an actor whisper when I would prefer he
spoke louder. I am not too critical. My future is held by these
strangers, whom I must trust. Failure is not an option.

Then there is opening night. I lean over my mother's bed
and tell her that the play is opening and that we are going to an
after party at a beautiful restaurant with peacock feathers on the
walls and the look of a Florentine garden. I tell her that in the
morning I will come and read her the reviews. I tell the child
who clings to my legs as I try to leave the house that this is
Daddy's big night, she must let me go. The babysitter pulls her
away and I hear her cries all the way down in the elevator, which
moves at its own pace despite my need to reach the ground floor
out of hearing, away from her despair.

Arthur Penn is in the back of the theater. Jack is sitting on
the stairs to the balcony. The curtain rises. The reviewers are in
their seats. The reviewer for the *New York Post* falls asleep. I can
see his chest heaving. The others seem attentive. They take
notes. At intermission Arthur Penn's wife squeezes my hand.

And then it is over. The audience has clapped warmly or so I
think. We are in the restaurant. Jack is like a ballet dancer
gracing all the tables at once, his tall form, his quick bright
smile, his drink in hand. Everyone is smoking, the air is hazy
through the light of the lamp on the wall. The publicist is there
and then a small television set is plugged in and we turn on the

evening news and the play reviewer speaks. He didn't like the play. He was bored. He found it pretentious. A silence settles over the room and then someone says, wait, wait for the papers, wait for *The New York Times*. And the chatter picks up and the glasses are raised in a toast to Arthur and Alfred and Jack. My stomach begins to turn.

Then about an hour later a man comes into the restaurant with the morning papers under his arm. And someone begins to read the reviews. One is more damning than the next. The actors are false, the play is without merit or meaning or humor. The play is imitative or dull and the endeavor a mistake. Soon the guests at the party collect their coats from the hat check and leave, and soon the restaurant empties and Jack tells me he is going out. Arthur and Peggy Penn rise to leave. It is not a triumph. There will be other plays, other opening nights. Arthur says good night to me, something in his manner tells me that he is saying goodbye, he is saying good luck. He is off, the cab door slams behind him. I go home alone. I want to take the child in bed with me for comfort, my comfort, but I resist. I stand at the window in the early hours of the day and watch the occasional car come down the street. The lights change and change again. Jack does not come home, not that day or the next or the one after that.

In the morning I go to tell my mother. I tell her that the reviews are mixed, a small white lie. She knows I am lying. She turns her head away from me in disgust, at my lie or at the play's failure I am not quite sure.

Jack has disappeared. He does not come back and the week

ends and another begins. Should I call the police, check the
hospitals or the morgues? I am at the window at two AM staring
down at the street below. The silence is broken once in a while
by a passing taxi, a car racing its motor. In the distance the
demanding sirens wail, a scrape of metal on metal as someone
out of sight rolls a garbage can against a lamppost. I can only see
the sky in a thin strip. A few stars out, a light that might be the
moon over a building roof, behind the black water tower with its
lace ladder rising upward. The play closed. Money, substantial
money has been lost. My mother is breathing and sleeping, but
her pulse is slow and every once in a while her body convulses,
cramps up, and grows stiff with small seizures, to be expected
the doctor said. The child wakes with a nightmare and I take her
into my bed where she curls against my side and returns to
sleep. What will happen to us now?

I imagine Jack leaning against a bar rail, his black hair damp
with sweat, his eyes red and small and his hands fluttering as he
talks to a woman whose makeup is thick and whose legs are long
and whose stockings are decorated with black lace. I imagine
her lipstick-stained cigarette and Jack producing dollars from an
inner pocket. I see him follow her out the door. I can smell her
perfume and the oils of her bath. I am not jealous. I hope she
soothes him. I know how he must feel, a man thrust out of
paradise, a man about to step on the top rock of Everest who has
suddenly been thrown by a wind down into a cavern far below
where his broken bones will prevent him from escape, where
fever and cold and starvation will soon bring him to death, a
death he has been expecting all along.

That is the moment I begin to despise the idea of fame. What does it do for the bearer of the laurel? Who cares if your name is in the paper? Who cares if you are mentioned as one of the top-ten cyclists, boxers, batters, painters, poets, artists, fly fishermen in the world? Who cares if your name is written in history books? When you have died you can't read those history books. When you have died the small trace you have left behind, even if you win a Tony, an Emmy, an Oscar, an election, will lose its vibrancy, fade into an outline. Oh yes, him, I heard of him, I knew someone who read him once. What difference does it make to the corpse if his books are in libraries or not in libraries? Who cares if his plays are revived on the summer-stock circuit for one hundred years? Isn't the simplest touch of a child's arm on the face more important, isn't the good meal, the brush against a thigh, a hand held during a movie, a swim in the sea, aren't those things of equal importance as the sands of time come rushing down on our heads burying ambition and love, good and evil, breath, blood, brains, waste, memory, alike in oblivion?

Jack wanted to be Michelangelo painting on the ceiling, lying on his back on the scaffolding. Good for Michelangelo. Good for us who stare up at the hand of God reaching toward Adam. But actually Michelangelo doesn't know that crowds line up and pay good money to enter the room to see his masterpiece, and if he had known, would his breakfast have tasted any better, his loves been any stronger, his life any longer? Would he have dined on a happiness of greater portion than the man who made a cabinet and sent it on to his patron's villa or the man who made puddings he sold from his cart? Fame is the snake in the garden, the great seducer. Perhaps Jack thought that if he were famous enough, enough like Keats, he could beat the hurt that chased him down dark streets or he might just sleep better at night.

The night of the bad reviews for his play was the night of a small assassination. I knew that each word cut his spirit, that no matter how hard he drank, how many packs of cigarettes he smoked, no matter what other drugs of highs or lows he found, these words seeped into his bloodstream, the pain would not lessen. No matter how many whores let him do this or that (and what did they do?), in the end he would be crushed, beyond repair. And so I grieved and began to hate the pursuit of fame and view it as a poison that withered my love and made me turn my face away from him in fear of his failure, which another man might have seen as a stumble on the path but I knew this man would see as a crash, as a cosmic condemnation, as a license to lie in bed all day and drink all night.

1955: There had always been a commune culture in America long before the hippies fled the urban centers to make bread in the dales of mountains in Vermont and Oregon. There were those Massachusetts Shakers who made beautiful furniture and prayed very sweetly to God but forgot that to endure on this planet you must reproduce your own. The Shakers, who found the sexual act too close to the Devil's pleasure, erased themselves in chastity, leaving behind a farm that turned into a museum and a very good cautionary tale for those of us who would survive. The world is not populated by saints because saints don't reproduce. If we imagine that little comets shooting across the sky are burning in pain for their God then we can see the saints taper out, leaving darkness, miles and miles of darkness behind. But America has had other communes that harvest and plant, have families that pray around communal tables, bake bread, avoid the cities, and form and dissolve like colonies of beavers on the river's edge. I went to one of these communes just before I met Jack.

My sociology professor had a pacifist son who had been a philosophy graduate student at Harvard when he joined a North Carolina commune with his young wife. It was to be his life, there in the hot fields with a pickup truck, fifty or so families, many of them the second or third generation to be raised on a commune. A small toy factory supported the commune. Some of the faces were peaceful faces and when they said to you God bless you, you knew they meant it, and even if you were a skeptic like me, you liked the way the words seemed like a handshake, like a gentle touch.

I went one day after Thanksgiving and stayed nearly two months. I thought I might stay forever but I had no mate and I grew bored and restless. Here there were no cashmere sweaters and no golf clubs in the closet. Here there were simple things, simple clothes, show was frowned on, ego was not considered a virtue, hard work was required, and love, everyone spoke all the time about love, God's, their own for you, yours for the plant you were tending, or the outhouse you were cleaning. I began to

smell an odor like that of sugar burning in the air at all times.
Reality was not a concern of these people. At each meal grace
was said, and said again as the plates were taken away to be
washed. There were long wooden tables in the dining house and
lists of jobs on the walls, and the sun streamed in the windows
and shined on the wood and everyone was grateful the baby
Jesus had been born, except me and maybe the philosophy
student who had quickly become the leader of the commune. In
his eyes I could see a certain discomfort, a holding back of his
prayer, a kind of doubt that made him blink too often, and while
he talked softly and said nothing harsh I felt he knew that the
banished reality of things was sure to return someday.

There was a lot of baking of bread and stewing of fruit and
boiling of things to put in jars. There was a lot of milking of
cows and dogs running everywhere and the crisp morning of
birdsong and wet grass underfoot and the purple-hued hills in
the distance and the sound of pickup trucks churning their
whining and undependable engines and the sight of men and
women painting eight-inch wooden horses with fine brushes and
leaning over tables to reach for the hand of a co-worker. Did
anyone there have bad dreams? Did anyone there have Freudian
dreams? I don't think so. Had anyone there heard of Freud, read
Beckett or Joyce or Mailer? Only the graduate student and he
wasn't about to admit it in public. I thought of Occam's razor.
The simplest explanation is the best. The truth is clean and
sharp and its lines are not twisted into barbed wire. But
sometimes simple is too simple.

And then there was the jazz musician, a sax player who had

been drunk in a bar in New Orleans when a schoolteacher found him, married him, and brought him to the commune. He had a ravaged face and he practiced his instrument with fingers tapping against the air whenever the music came into his ears. He was alive like a nasty wire sparking, cut from the others. One night he stole a truck and went somewhere and didn't come back at dawn or at lunch or in time for evening prayers. The leader of the commune and some others went off to find him and their truck that he had taken and they found him in a bar in a nearby town and brought him back and sobered him up and kept him locked in a house while every few hours a different commune member went to see him and pray with him and bring him back to God. He escaped through a window. I hope forever. There is the totalitarian side of utopia. There is no utopia.

However, I wanted to live there with the smell of cow manure, the brisk cool of morning, the sun on the fields, the flowers that grew by the path, the love of man for woman and woman for man, and the softness of the sky with its stars so visible it was possible to believe there was after all a plan, a purpose, a reason for things. But words from my real life kept rising up in my mind, insistent like Hamlet's ghost. I heard them at night and in the pauses in conversation, in the moments I rested after cleaning or washing or cooking. The words said, "hysteria," they said, "delusions," when the commune leaders denied that one of the caretakers of the children was coughing up blood and drenched in sweat from a fever. My voices said, "wishful thinking," they said, "boredom," they said, "nonsense."

They asked, "What would Proust have to say about this group of souls?" They asked, "What would Freud think?" The words of civilization spread discontent in my brain like the spherules of syphilis gorging on the neurons and synapses of a hapless victim.

I remember most clearly the lunchtime when I was sitting at a long table next to the graduate student's wife, who had been at Radcliffe and dropped out. She was a large young woman with braids that lay across her considerable bosom or were roped around her head. She wore big dresses and had arms freckled from the sun. She smelled of grass and wheat and her eyes had a faraway look as if she were not quite there, listening perhaps to something more important that was drifting through the air. After the plates were cleared and before the final prayer she rose and moved to the center of the room. She began to dance. "God is speaking to me," she said and she waved her arms and sank to the floor and rose again and I could see from her pale remote face that she was not quite in the room. She said she was dancing His words. She said she could hear Him whisper in her ear. She was crazy, I thought. She whirled around and stamped at the floor and hummed into the room, a wordless hum that became a scream without a distinct word, a scream that was angry but was meant as a prayer and others clapped and pounded the table to her rhythm and I sat there wondering if she needed to be taken to a hospital. And then I tried to hear her. I tried to let the dance reach my soul. She was heavy and ungraceful, but earnest in her gestures, and I believed if I tried hard enough I might lift myself from myself. How good that would be. But I didn't. Instead I began to wonder if she should be left to care for the children of the commune when her turn came, perhaps she shouldn't drive a truck to town to get supplies. I wondered if she might not be dangerous. I was also embarrassed by the nakedness of her desire to be close to God. Like the jazz musician, I danced to another tune.

I drove back to New York City with another student, a would-be poet. Somewhere in Delaware he pulled into a rest stop. He put gas into the car. He bought us both sodas and then he said he wanted to have sex with me. He had earned it by driving such a long distance. He took out his notebook and read me his poems. He too yearned for God. I was tired of God. I was all sweaty and not so clean. You pay for everything, I figured.

When I got back to college I stayed in the shower a long time.

I HEARD a few years later that the commune had dissolved because one of the members had backed his truck out onto the main road and had killed a four-year-old child who was playing in the patch of grass where the truck turned. And the death of the child broke the spell. No one wanted to be there anymore and the lifetime members of the commune left to find other communes and the new residents returned to their old lives and the philosophy graduate student completed his thesis and went to teach at a university in the Midwest and he became a union organizer or a professor of political science, perhaps both.

A decade later there were communes everywhere. A decade later the communes were not so much focused on the goodness of God but on the goodness of sex, but I imagine the difference was not as important as it might seem. The important matter would have been the baking of bread, the chopping of herbs, the smell of a new morning, the sense of virtue that could become the vice of smugness in an eyeblink. So many were seeking a better way, an escape from what so clearly had not worked for parents in the suburbs, parents in the cities, parents who divorced, parents who drank, parents who wandered the earth, waiting on the train platforms for their commuter trains, a search for something that claimed to provide freedom, claimed to be a way to escape the normal disappointments, a way to avoid the modern condition. It turned out there was no way to avoid human foulness—it follows right into the countryside and sleeping with anyone you like creates a kind of chaos that leaves the same bitter taste as never sleeping with anyone you like. As Jean-Paul Sartre said, "No exit."

1961: Arthur Penn had a house in Stockbridge, Massachusetts. Tennessee Williams and William Inge were both at the prominent psychiatric hospital Austen Riggs in the Berkshires at the same time. Near Stockbridge is where Edith Wharton's large Victorian house still stands and readers make pilgrimages to walk on the same lawn she walked and crunch the same fall leaves, the reds and oranges and yellows that fell from the oaks and maples and elms when she was there dreaming of escape to another continent. There is a New England inn there called the Red Lion and winding roads up steep hills and Austen Riggs, expensive Austen Riggs, had

famous psychiatrists walking its halls and patients who stayed
months and years, some to return to waiting husbands and
wives, some to struggle with alcohol and dark thoughts until
their usually premature ends. Tennessee Williams and William
Inge had written plays that brought them fortune and fame. The
attention that followed did not heal the split in the heart that
drove them each day to doubt the worth of their lives, and they
sank as some do into a slough of despond, a place that has a
poetic name but is in fact closer to the sewer facilities that
gathered beneath old-fashioned outhouses and now have
become the rivers of waste that run day and night under our
cities, out of sight, protected by grates and bars, so it is hard to
fall in unless you try.

Austen Riggs did their best but the affliction of gift came at a
price, a high price. I thought perhaps Austen Riggs would save
Jack. He wasn't interested. I had no money to send him there. I
dreamed of it though, the city on the hill with psychiatrists on
call and the snow falling on peaceful farms and Edith Wharton's
spirit watching over the writers of another century. There
presidents of Harvard and headmasters of Groton were buried in
a circle in an old cemetery up a mountain road. Emerson was
sane. Emily Dickinson at least was not a drunk. But I was
grasping at straws.

Were all these writers and artists more fragile than ordinary
human beings or do we just know their names? It does seem as if
there is a peril associated with gift, a proclivity to break your
brain just as professional skiers may be apt to break their legs as
they swoop downward through wind and snow. It may be that to

see and tell the story of human error is to dare to expose yourself to the sacred flash of truth that can drive you mad. Or are you mad to try in the first place?

1963: And then Jack left the apartment with a suitcase. He came back and took his books, and he left me the paperback French editions with the sweet-smelling glue in the bindings, Racine, Descartes, Hugo, Voltaire. I gave him the couch and the armchair and the lamps my mother had bought. I didn't want them. I gave him the rug and the china figurines my aunt had given me as a wedding present. I didn't want them. He had already pawned the silverware, the art deco salad servers, the amethyst my aunt had given me on my eighteenth birthday. The gold circle pin my mother gave me when I delivered the child. He took the antique clock and the French nineteenth-century chair my mother had bought him for his twenty-fifth birthday.

IT HAPPENED this way. Some weeks after his Broadway play closed he did come back. He slept all day and left again each night. We hardly talked. Finally I invited a few friends over for dinner in hopes his spirits would recover. Someone brought a young actress and her actor brother and her father, an Italian writer, who told me that he had been working in Rome on his novel for five years and finally finished the manuscript and took the train to Paris to bring the manuscript to his publisher there. I imagined the man, his gray-speckled long hair and his sensitive lips and the cigarettes he smoked and the landscape flying by.

There he is floating in the joy of completion, the anticipation of praise from his editor, adoration from his readers. There he is silencing the nagging anxiety within—will there be another book, does he have an idea or has the well run dry? There he is wondering if he is as good as he wants to be. Would the Princess Caetani print an excerpt in her magazine? Would the papers interview him in his favorite café? The signs with the names of the towns appear and disappear one after another as the train heads north toward Paris. And then he arrives and gathers his coat and his hat and his little overnight bag and he leaves on the rack above his seat the briefcase that carries his manuscript and when he arrives at his little hotel on the rue de Lille he realizes the manuscript is gone and he takes a taxi back to the train station but the train has already left for its return to Rome. He has the stationmaster cable ahead but the conductor searches in the car, above the seat and below the seat, and cannot find the manuscript or any sign of a briefcase, black with a torn edge on the right side and a tarnished clasp that sometimes comes undone. And the work is gone and I hear this story and the author's hand is shaking as he swallows his bourbon and water in quick gulps. I am appalled. How could he leave the train without the pages that he had worked on for so long? There were in those days no photocopy machines, no memory sticks, nothing but the single typed manuscript, and perhaps a carbon if one was patient and set it right. This manuscript had no carbon. It was lost forever. Everyone knew that one of Hemingway's wives had left his manuscript on a train. It was a famous story with a moral I understood: Be kind to your wife or don't let your manuscript out of your sight. Wait a minute. Was my Italian writer telling me a true story or had he simply decided to awe a naïve American woman with a shopworn tale from the literary archives which sometimes resembled the gossip pages of the local tabloids?

The Italian writer had come to America with his children to start again. And as the conversations around the room grew louder with the lateness of the hour and the kitchen sink overflowed with empty bottles, I saw Jack leaning over the young actress, describing something to her with his hands on her shoulders. He was obvious. I was embarrassed. He kissed her neck. She blushed. I turned away. I wasn't jealous in the usual sense. He did not want her any more than he wanted me. He was playing for the watching eyes. He was playing to assuage his pride. He was like a wounded toreador headed for another pass at the bull but bleeding under his shirt. Her hair was soft and straight and her eyes were alive with the wonder of the grown-up world and its antics and I felt old and tired and ready for bed. The child would wake in a few hours. I was jealous of her life, of the conquests she would surely make.

Later I saw him put on his coat and fetch hers from the child's room where it lay on a couch and I saw them leave. The other guests saw this too. I noticed the half-amused pity in their eyes when they looked at me.

AND THEN AS IF someone turned out the light, my marriage was over. It was a pretend marriage anyway. I was twenty-seven and old and I had failed. And Jack said he could not stay any longer. He moved out within the week.

I have no pity for her, the still-young woman helping her fleeing husband pack his shirts into a suitcase that had belonged to her mother. I have no pity for that about-to-be-divorced woman who had been ready to live off the written words of someone else.

I called a filmmaker friend, Eleanor Perry, and her husband, Frank, and asked if they would come over. I needed company. "Yes," they said, after a party they had to attend, some Hollywood agent was in town. I waited until one in the morning for my doorbell to ring. They didn't come. I understood. The party had moved on.

1960: I have been married to Jack for three years. I am nine months pregnant. It is December and it's snowing, a real snow that is piling up against the tires of the parked cars, that's swirling above the traffic lights and leaving drifts high against the curbs. I am walking along Third Avenue to pick up Jack's typewriter, which needed some part replaced. It is ready and he is sleeping and I do not want him to be without his typewriter when he awakes. The store is still open. The man behind the counter gives me the typewriter and I set off with it in my arms wrapped in a protective cover. It is heavy. I lean it against my protruding stomach. There are no buses running. I am about fifteen blocks from our building. I see no taxis. The storm is growing stronger. Suddenly I feel a wetness down my leg. The water has broken. I need to go to the hospital. I rest the typewriter on a car fender and consider what to do. I struggle on.

I make it several blocks. I stop at a pay phone. Jack is sleeping and he doesn't wake up. I walk on to the hospital. It's another twenty blocks. I will not leave the typewriter behind. I am afraid I will give birth in the snow. I do not. From the hospital pay phone I call my mother.

THERE HAD NEVER been a moment in my conscious life when I was not planning on becoming a writer. That is why I was reading, that is why I was trying to hear the low hum of reality under the disguises it so cleverly donned. I wanted to report on the crimes of unloving parents and betraying lovers and the things that went on in the dark where I could not see. But from the first trip across the Fifty-ninth Street Bridge with Jack I lost the desire to write. I wanted Jack to write the words that he could write. I wanted him to take his place in the firmament of stars. I thought he would outshine Joyce and I thought I had found my place, which was to type his manuscripts carefully, to put them in envelopes and mail them to editors here and there. How did it happen that I gave up so quickly, without a word on paper, my ambition? It may be that I feared that as a female I had no subject. I knew of course of Virginia Woolf and George Eliot and Jane Austen but they seemed so foreign, so of another place, that they did not so much inspire me as remind me that I was an ordinary person, from an ordinary world, more crass than elegant, more wanting of genius than not.

I had never known a woman doctor or a woman lawyer. They existed of course but not in sufficient numbers for me to have known them. I had read Mary McCarthy and Willa Cather but they seemed so other to me. However, I cannot blame my failure to begin on a discouraging world. It was more likely the kind of balk that occurs when a horse gallops up to the jump and stops in his tracks. I also knew and know now that Jack was a better writer than I could ever be and that he had a sharper mind than I had. I didn't want to be mediocre. What was this lust for greatness that afflicted me? It was in the air, yes. But not everyone was vulnerable to its siren call. Perhaps the ambition was in opposite proportion to one's place on the social scale or perhaps the more one felt unattached to the American pyramid the more one needed to perch at the top. Or maybe the fifties themselves drove its outsiders to absurd lengths so we wouldn't be washed away into the rivers of banality.

1963: I took the child to the park. While she slept in her stroller I drank coffee in a local diner. I thought, I must do something. I reread *Remembrance of Things Past* but that was not doing anything. I was invited to the ongoing Friday-night party at George Plimpton's. Now I was a single woman. Jack would be there but it didn't matter. I went. That was doing something. And in addition I bought a notebook. The kind of small square black notebook I had used in high school. It had lines and margins inked in red. I began to tell the story of my family although I made up all sorts of things. I made up names and invented fictions to make my point. I wrote when the child was asleep. I wrote when she was at nursery school. I could tell that I was not polite on the page. I was a nasty writer. Why had it taken so long for me to get started? Yes I was swimming against the cultural tide. Yes I needed earplugs to block the voice within that chided and scoffed and pointed out how little of the world I understood and how clumsy my sentences were. But those are just excuses. It took me a long time to start, to remember that I had always wanted to write the story of my life, even when I had not yet reached double digits. I too had to learn that it wasn't necessary to be the best at what you do. I too had to tolerate fear of failure and a sense of diminishment that came into this world with my genitals. I had to learn that muses can be fired or dismissed but writers either do or don't write without permission or encouragement from anyone. I did begin. I told the child I was writing a book. She offered to draw the pictures.

I didn't care anymore if all the writers in America were more skilled than I. I began to write because I was no longer concerned about my lack of great gift. I would work with whatever lay within. It was a secret, this notebook of mine. I described things. I remembered scenes. I wrote about the child and what she did. I wrote about my mother and my father and my aunts and my uncles. I wrote the stories my mother had told me about her father and his first years on the Lower East Side. I wrote in the supermarket. I wrote while the child napped. I wrote when the child was crayoning or listening to music.

WE ARE AT the main beach in East Hampton. I have made a new friend and her husband is an actor. She is friends with Adolph Green and Phyllis Newman and they know all the theater people around. They have a little boy my child's age. Phyllis Newman has a niece who is a plump sweet-faced New Jersey girl who has come to visit, and I hear Phyllis say to her niece, "Do not marry an ordinary man, you will have an ordinary boring life. You need to find a special man with great talent so you can be a part of the electricity of the world." I am, by now, not so sure. Are great men such good companions? I've been to the party. Who cares about the big apartment on Central Park West and the openings and the songs and the producers from Hollywood calling and the agents sending you bouquets of flowers if in the middle of the night you still get the shakes and if you put out a hand and no one is there to take it? The stars in my eyes are burning out.

1964: A wild rain is beating against the windowpanes. I see smears of red and green on the street as the traffic lights change and the iron fences on the islands of Park Avenue shimmer against the dark brush behind them. The phone rings. It is Frank Perry. He is in town and wants to come see me after his business dinner. We are friends. He had not forgotten me. I am pleased. He arrives with two dozen roses. It is after eleven. He sits next to me on the couch. He takes my hand and leads me into the bedroom. "But Eleanor," I protest. He ignores me. He is a large man with a wide chest. He wants me. I tell him to be quiet because the child is asleep in the next room. He is not so quiet. When he leaves I throw out the roses. I am in a John O'Hara story. I am in a John Cheever story. I don't like the plot.

I want someone to watch over me and not just when they happen to be in town.

1961: I am at the beach with my child who is in diapers. She is walking and talking and she sits down on the lap of a man on the blanket I am sitting on. The man is Jason Robards and next to him is the love of his life, Lauren Bacall. The child sits happily for a second on Jason's lap and he kisses her cheek. The child says loudly and clearly, "I smell scotch. Where is the bottle?" Jason laughs, but he is embarrassed. It is not yet noon. I am embarrassed. I scoop the child up and go down to the water's edge. How many sixteen-month-old children recognize the smell of scotch on the breath?

1963: The child likes to sing and dance and she drinks in applause as if she has found the only oasis in the great expanse of desert that surrounds her. Adam Green, the son of Adolph and Phyllis, is also a performer. We are sitting on the patio and the two children under four years of age decide to perform for us. They start to sing together. They have rehearsed. Suddenly my child pushes Adam out of the center of the circle. Pushes until he retreats. She stands in the center of the circle and finishes the song. I grab her to say you cannot do this. But Phyllis laughs and says, "Yes she can, that's show business." I don't want my child to behave like that. "Good for her," says Adolph, "she knows what you have to do." I don't want my child to be a saint walking barefoot in villages on distant continents but a little civility seems like a good idea. I see how thirsty she is for the sun to shine on her and her alone and I worry.

I think of the theater as if it were Jack the Ripper leaning into the shadows, following discreetly behind, until the moment comes and a knife is drawn out from a loose cloak and blood is drawn on the cobblestones and mingles with the sewage drifting in the gutter. Perhaps this is a melodramatic way to refer to drama critics, producers, stars, folk of the late night.

1964: The following summer, or was it the summer after, when I am no longer with Jack and have rented a small house behind the railroad tracks, Phyllis gives her niece a wedding. The man was not famous or even especially promising as far as I knew and the caterers came and set up on the lawn and as they were cooking the wedding feast a gas canister exploded and a fire started and the entire house was in flames and the wedding guests fled. I wasn't there. I heard many stories about the event. I thought it was a metaphor, but exactly for what I wasn't sure. If the niece had married a movie star would the house have burned down? Was this God's comment on marriage in general or in the specific? It was certainly theatrical.

I go to a party at a small house in East Hampton. We can smell the ocean from the front porch. There are chairs on the lawn and candles in glass jars are set on small tables. There is a writer of a memoir. His name is Frank Conroy. And he's married

to a high-school friend of mine, a tall dusty-haired gangly woman with a shy smile, round glasses, and a long classical face that speaks of a childhood at horse shows, on basketball courts, on hockey teams. She is the granddaughter of Judge Learned Hand. She has rectitude in her posture, the pallor of the just, and now her eyes are sad and she seems out of place among the flamboyant and the drunk and those whose parents never heard of society's blue book. There she is, intelligent and stranded among those with wild hair and bare feet, and Tessa smoking on a swing in the yard. Frank Conroy is a friend of my ex-husband and Jack is there too, his arms around a young girl who refills his glass as soon as it is empty.

My high-school friend and I had spent hours together mostly smoking and sipping at ice-cream sodas. I envied her Oriental rugs, a living room with a portrait of a nineteenth-century relative hanging above the sofa, her mother with sensible shoes and a life of volunteering for good causes. She did not invite me to her coming-out party at the Piping Rock Country Club but I understood. And then here she is, a Radcliffe graduate (or was it Vassar?), married to a writer, a brilliant writer, a drunken writer, who is the father of her boys. Just like me, she fell. Had I harmed her in our conversations as we walked to school, had I diverted her from safer destinies or was it not my fault?

I wanted to talk to Frank Conroy. I wanted to watch Frank Conroy from across the porch. There was great woe in his shoulders, in the lines in his young face, in the slightly cold eyes that lit up when he talked about jazz, I could hear him from across the floor. I could see why she married him but I knew by then that time would separate them. On that porch there were no stories with happy endings.

I had asked Jack to call me if he was coming to East Hampton and I told him I hoped he would come by to see the child and I would drive anywhere to pick him up if he wished. I told him I did not want the child surprised by seeing him with other people. What would she think? She was old enough to be thinking. And so I am on the beach walking with the child looking for shells to paint. There is a fishing boat on the horizon and I show the child how the nets are down and I show her the terns that dash away as we approach and I tell her that when she is bigger I will take her out into the deep waves to dive beneath, when just ahead of me I see Frank Conroy and his wife and behind them their sons, and along with them I see Carol Southern and Jack, his pale thin chest and dark sunglasses to hide his red-flecked eyes and a bathing suit slipping down on his thin hips, and on Jack's shoulders, towering above us all, I see Niles Southern. So does the child. There is an awkward moment on the beach as we meet. The child stares up at Niles. We all nod and smile. The child turns away and runs into the water. The waves are lapping up on her legs. I go after her. "Daddy is visiting," I say. "He'll call and come by later," I say. He doesn't. "Daddy would come to see me if I were a boy like Niles," she says several days later. "No, no," I say. But what can I say? How to explain to a child that Daddy doesn't care about Niles either or Carol? He cares about Frank Conroy and about Terry Southern and about being a great writer, not a failed playwright, sinking under the waves of anonymity. I want to tell the child that Daddy is hurt but I don't know if I should or shouldn't. I don't.

I understand. Jack needs and cannot give. I need and can give. But what I can give he does not need and what I need he cannot give. I have harmed my child. The child is caught, not in the middle, there is no middle, she is caught with me. For the first time in my adult life I see that it may be sufficient for a person who loves the written word to simply read. The actual authors of those words may be on fire and fire burns. The alcohol consumed is meant to put out the flame but it serves instead as an accelerant.

1963–1964: In the fall I go to George Plimpton's. The night is long and the married women with young children have left to go to bed so that they can rise with their children. I am talking to William Styron. He is bleary. He lives in Connecticut. He is broad and his face has a beaten-up look, circles under his eyes, his chest wide and he leans out to me. I want to go to bed with you, he says. Why not, I say. Why not anything? Does he want to go to bed with me because I understand and admire his books? I don't think so. Does he want to go to bed with me because I am appealing and warm-breasted and dark-haired and not entirely stupid? I don't think so. I can see that he wants to go to bed with me because he needs to go to bed and soon before he passes out and he wants to go to bed with me because I am there, in the first hours of the new day with the other men sprawled on couches and chairs and I am still awake and I have an apartment to go to, and I am someone whom he knows as one of the crowd, Jack Richardson's ex-lady, and he has a Southern mewl that makes me think for a moment that he might desire me and that in the vast ebb and flow of time, Stone Age to now, desire is a constant and ought not to be ignored because what else have we, I agree. His breath is heavy with nicotine and so much alcohol I wonder that his tongue isn't on fire. Yes, I think, he is a wonderful writer. Yes, I think, he is a stranger from another place where magnolia hangs heavy on trees and dark crimes are different from the dark crimes I know. I look in his eyes and I see Faulkner and sweat pouring off shoulders lifting bales of cotton and Scarlett and Rhett and I think I see a stripe of blood across his back when he turns over in bed. I don't mind that he rises in the morning and puts on his pants and his shirt and tie and grabs his jacket without waiting for a cup of coffee. He has to return to Connecticut. He says he has a wife and children and he has a typewriter up there and pages more to go. Also he has bottles of his favorite aphrodisiac stored in his study. I am like a glass left on the bar, empty, a lipstick stain on the rim, a melted ice cube at the bottom. It is not yet dawn when he leaves and I stand in the doorway and wait with him for the elevator. He taps his foot impatiently. I wonder if he will come back. A few more times, late at night we found each other as the room was emptying out and George was already in his room with the door closed with some sweet girl with hopes he might offer her a job on *The Paris Review* and he does know my address and gives it to the cabdriver without my help. I try to say interesting things to him. His eyes are always far away as if he were staring at me across a muddy river where the mist never lifts. He has certain feelings about Jewish girls. He married one after all. He likes our ferocity, I suspect. But then he doesn't like competing with the Jewish writers who stomped onto the stage without asking leave, writers like Mailer and Malamud and Bellow. He does not like the righteousness of the Jewish writer or the taint of slavery that follows him, an innocent Southerner, about. That I learn when reading *Sophie's Choice* more than a decade later.

One Friday night at George's, the ethnic drama breaks out. The gladiators each have their supporters. Out on the landing just in front of George's apartment voices are raised, a crowd begins to gather. Norman Mailer attempts to hit Doc Humes and the two are fighting on the stairwell. I am there watching. Doc thinks Norman has sold out to the FBI. I think Norman suspects someone is after his money or his rights or his name. Someone said an ugly thing. George is standing between them, bending a little because he is taller than the others. He tries to joke. He puts a friendly hand on one shoulder or the other but as if two bulls were pawing the ground the air becomes steamy and thick and the cigarette smoke swirls above and Norman has already put a penknife in his wife Adele's belly after a party and Doc Humes, a Ferdinand if ever there was one, suddenly has an enraged look in his eye. I turn away. I don't want to get testosterone poisoning. I don't remember how it stopped. Norman was tougher, but Doc was crazier. Others separated them perhaps before a single blow landed. I know that the writers who witnessed the fight all thought of ways to write about it. I know that in a place where it was understood that manhood needed to be earned over and over again and could be taken away from a contender at any minute, the actual prize should have gone to George who really didn't want blood on his stairwell. Did he understand that Norman was the intruder from the immigrant Jewish side of the street and Doc was the defender from the old family that took America for granted? Did he know that all the women there were like the flowers on the tables at a wedding, wilting, waiting to be thrown out?

Afterward there was talk and more talk about the fight. It grew to mythical proportions, constellations in the sky were named after the encounter. Odd that. A real war had taken place in all our childhoods—a war in Korea had taken old friends and left them rotting on scrubby hills one identical to another. Many of the men in the room were veterans of that war which they, just like their older brothers, did not want to talk about, not ever. The death of us all waited in the muscles of an itchy finger on a cool button under a distant mountain. And yet we were riveted by the tale of Norman Mailer and Doc Humes late at night on the stairwell of George Plimpton's apartment. I thought of the encounter as if the *Tyrannosaurus rex* and his archenemy had danced around each other on a primitive plain, one on which the other beasts gathered and were holding martinis in their claws.

"Do not go gentle into that good night," said the poet Dylan Thomas, which is a lovely line, encouraging the human spirit against the gravity of death which certainly had that drinker in its grip. Actually the writers gathered at George's for an evening of pleasure and pain did not want to go gentle into the next day, never mind the coffin. These kings of the hill were jostling for prizes named and unnamed and sometimes I was one of those prizes, which was fine with me.

1964: Orgies. Well, it was the sixties. There was a fellow who was a friend of George's who arranged the orgies. He had an Irish name. He was the barker at the current circus. Chris Worth went to the orgies and he wanted to take me. But I was afraid. What was I afraid of? I still thought in a corner of my mind that sex without love was corrupting of the heart. I thought that I would be stained by sex without affection. But I had already had such sex and had not noticed any change in my body or mind. Everyone else lent their bodies for this or that occasion and looked exactly the same the next morning. Still I considered it unholy. I considered myself unholy and didn't want to further lose my way. I had no acceptable reason for my reluctance. I did not believe in purity of body and soul and I saw so little fidelity around me that I could no more believe in it than I could insist that unicorns roamed Central Park in the hours before dawn.

If I was going to live life to its wildest edge I considered that I might have to undress in front of strangers and let my body be touched and touch others in ways that made me feel as if I were living inside a Bosch painting, strange-shaped hunchbacks, gnomes, snakes with bulging eyes all rubbing against my naked skin.

My avoidance of the actual orgy can be looked at two ways. The first reason sees me as a coward, a cultural coward, a good girl with her mother's voice in her head, "No one will marry you if you're not a virgin." The first condemns me for standing at the brink of freedom and backing off, a woman who can't take things as they come but is looking for familiarity, security, a dull woman who will lose her chance to taste euphoria.

The second reason: I stood at the door of George Plimpton's early one morning and grabbed my coat before the action started. I was protecting the child from the chaos that was coming. I was looking not for more sweat and tingle and joy but for constancy and caring and a partner for a home that would make the child safe. The second reason was that I needed not a dozen hands on my breasts but one pair, one that might become familiar, dear. I had not given up that hope and the rooms filled with thrashing limbs seemed to lead me in another direction away from what I really wanted.

Or was I just a coward—a girl seeking a white picket fence in suburban Connecticut, station wagon a must. I was afraid of the dark—that is true. I pulled back from the fire when I thought I might get singed. Or was I a prude? Which of my reasons was the true reason? I never found the answer. The orgies went on without me.

Of course George's evenings without the formal orgy had a certain unhinged quality. After many of the women went home, after the less well known, the outer-circle men, the hangers-on, who were greeted warmly but not exactly a part of the inner crowd, after they had left, the remaining men and women draped themselves together on couches, on chairs, on whatever bed could be found. The jackets were off. The ties sometimes lay beside a lamp or next to a bookcase. The ice was melted in the bucket and words were slurred. Someone vomited in the bathroom. There was a lot of whispering and the sound of a soft moan from a bedroom or a nearby couch. The lights seemed to be dimmer. An old prep-school friend had passed out on the floor and the women who stayed—and if my babysitter would stand for it, I stayed—were apt to leave their bras behind the couch cushions or stuff them into their pocketbooks. Lipstick was applied and reapplied and red-stained tissues sat about the sink. Once I lost my watch and found it several Friday nights later under a couch along with a crumpled napkin and an old piece of cheese now covered with a green mold.

Sometimes I see Chris Worth. He does have a broad face. He does have a wide chest. But that was not his appeal. It was the way he knew it was not a joke even when he pretended it was. It was the way he knew that something more important mattered but it was not right to mention the more important thing. It was the way I knew he knew who I was even without my telling him. But he was married and had children and he left my house in the early morning and I wouldn't see him again for a few weeks and when I did I knew I shouldn't let him near me. But he was the beautiful unicorn in my imaginary garden. He was blond. He was Aryan. He didn't want to kill me. Is that a sufficient reason to love someone? I didn't pine for him. There would have been no point. I didn't have dreams of running away to California with him. I did love the way he ruffled my hair, which needed no ruffling. I did believe he was a man who deserved to ski down mountain trails in the winter and sail across the bay at his yacht club's annual Labor Day race, summer following summer, because there was no evil in him, no unkindness waiting for its moment, a large man with an ironic smile, I liked his touch. The last time I saw him was at a beach picnic. The bonfires were lit, the little glowworms flickered neon-green in the sand. The parking lot lay dark behind us. He was a good thing in a world of fevered men crashing about and kissing other women in the dunes. They say that for every person there is a fated one, a perfect match. In Hebrew it is called one's *beshert*. Not true. One has many fated ones in a lifetime and fate is a wild joker anyway.

And then one night George turned to me and began telling me a story about André Gide and Paul Claudel and how they had an argument about the existence of God and the day after Claudel died a telegram arrived for Gide and it said *"Dieu existe."* And then we looked around the room and it was late and mostly everyone had left and George asked me if he could come back with me and I said yes. It wasn't a huge Molly Bloom kind of yes but it was sufficient and we sat in the taxi and he put his hands up my skirt and I wasn't sorry. His upper-class accent, his tall athletic handsomeness, his big hands and feet, the way he had to bend down to touch my ear were all appealing. My people may have come off boats and been despised by his people in their time but now I was present in my black silk party dress, my dark European visions of murder and exile dancing in my head, going home in a cab with a man whose parents belonged to clubs that closed their doors to mine. The man who owned the hand climbing up my thigh came from parents who had played tennis for generations and tacked in and out of the wind on little boats. Generations of his people had learned sportsmanship at schools that led to entrance to other schools where there were more clubs that would close their doors to me and mine. But here I was, and the mouth from which the fine accent came was pressing itself against mine, and there was a red lipstick stain on his face, my lipstick, and I thought to myself, I wonder if he likes me. It doesn't matter, I thought. He doesn't, I thought. I don't care, I thought and took him upstairs to bed.

And a few hours later I woke to feel small hands on my face. It was the child. George was asleep, his long body almost hanging off my bed. The child said, "Who is that?" and put a small finger on his nose. "That," I said, "is my friend George." She looked at him carefully. "Does he have a penis," she said. "Probably," I said. "Let's look," she said. The sky was pale white and the sun was just appearing over the Triborough Bridge. The child pulled back the covers. "Yes," she said, "he has a penis." George stirs. He sees the child. "Oh God," he says. "What is her name again?" I tell him. He closes his eyes and turns his back. Have I traumatized the child? I feel a pain in my chest. Am I having a heart attack? I carry her back into her bed and sit by her side until she falls asleep. I have sinned. Not in the religious sense but in the psychoanalytic sense. Primal scene—early exposure to strangers' organs, a string of men, a long line of groping hands on her mother's breasts. I stare at the coming morning. An ambulance shrieks along the avenue. I am ashamed. How is it possible for a mother to harm the child who gives her a reason to live? I am the one thing in the world I had vowed never to be, a mother with a bad conscience. I deserved my life.

The alarm rings. I get up and dress. George stirs in bed, rises, showers, and dresses, puts on his jacket and tie. He shaves with my razor. He looks new and clean and there are no shadows under his eyes. A night of sin leaves him dewy and refreshed. I offer to make him coffee but he refuses. He says to me, a kind of apology in his voice, "If I see you in a few years I might have forgotten I slept with you." "That's all right," I say. But I didn't forget and he did.

I wait with him at the elevator until it arrives. Behind me in the kitchen, the child is spilling cereal on the floor in great handfuls, hoping for my attention. I turn and shut the door. I have only half an hour to get the child to nursery school.

Of course there exists an entire universe between virginity and promiscuity. Yes, there is a concept in Western culture of moderation. We need that cautionary concept precisely because so many of us are not drawn to the mean. Moderation for most of us is a most unnatural condition despite promising comfort, despite offering less danger than the extremes. In moderation's wake follows kindness and safety, calm and thoughtfulness. Also it can be dull, droning dull.

I preferred to burn out like a brilliant firecracker, red, blue, green points of light shooting into the night sky, than to live like my mother's pearls resting in a velvet box on a satin cushion waiting for something I had no power to imagine. True, no one

was asking me to climb into a velvet box and rest for a hundred
years but that did not affect my choice, which of course was
artificial, peculiar, and romantic in the worst sense of the word. I
began to think of moving away, the Canadian Rockies, Hawaii,
Samoa, Montana. I imagined that I might find a better life for
the child if I went away, far away. But my mind was careening
about like a hungry hamster in a cage. If I were a firecracker in
the Limberlost I might burn the forest down or, worse, fizzle out
in a pile of pine needles unseen. Anyway I went nowhere.

1962: I did think it prudent to leave the city with the
child the weekend of the Cuban missile crisis. I did believe that
the end could be upon us. I looked in her wide hopeful eyes and
felt despair that she wouldn't have time to grow, to grow to be
better than her mother. I called the airlines to book a flight to
Montreal. There were no seats available, none for Chicago or
Corpus Christi. I called the railroad. There were no tickets to
Canada, no tickets to Albany, no tickets to Washington, D.C. I
could have gone to California I suppose, or perhaps St. Louis.
But I didn't think of it. I waited like everyone else and thought of
a radioactive sky and bananas soaked in atoms and I thought that
I would die with the child in my arms and I would tell her that
everything would be fine even though I knew it wouldn't. And
then the boats turned back.

Why didn't I walk out of the city with the child on my back?
Why didn't I just go to the highway and hitch a ride to North
Carolina? I don't know. When it was over I was unimpressed

with my survival skills but promised myself to act faster, to be bolder, for the sake of the child, next time around.

1965: I begin to worry about supporting the child. What if I remain a single woman and I have no profession? I begin graduate school at New York University in sociology. I will be a sociologist and study the ways of men in groups. I will become wise and sharp.

I GO TO East Hampton for the summer with the child. I have an au pair from Sweden. She has a boyfriend who paints in the garage of the small house I have rented. He paints large canvases with black stripes. He gives the child rides on his shoulders and he lifts cases of beer into the house which he drinks with the au pair in the evenings while I go out with someone or other I have met on a beach blanket, someone I have met at a cocktail party. The child screams in terror when I go out. I see that I have done something wrong. I always come back. I tell the child I always come back, but in her eyes I see the look of a wild animal facing the hunters whose intentions are not good. I tell the child I will read her one more story and I do, but I feel her fingers on my wrist digging in, holding on as if I were a life raft slipping away from its mooring. I know I cannot live like a mayfly anymore. I know that I must find a life, one life, and choose it for my child, and the title of a Thomas Mann story keeps going through my head, "Disorder and Early Sorrow." I repeat the words to myself as I pack a lunch to take to

the beach, as I drive my car home in the early hours of the
morning along the Montauk highway where Jackson Pollock has
killed himself and his ghost can be seen in my reflector lights
when the fog is not too thick. I am disordered and have early
sorrow. I have given my child early sorrow and too much
disorder. She grasps at the hand of every man who pauses at our
blanket on the beach. She dances and sings and smiles at
everyone. She is hoping that she can find a daddy since I have
failed.

Terry Southern is in California with some lady, I am sure, or
perhaps his only lady is the dope he has begun to sell along the
coast or so I am told. Jed Gelber knocks down the child's castle
and screams in rage when his ice cream falls into the sand.
Tessa's husband is planning to leave her soon, he says his analyst
thinks that would be best. Tessa wakes at noon and is sad until
nightfall. Her analyst thinks her stay as a refugee child without
parents has made her vulnerable to pain. Her analyst thinks she
should go back to work. Tessa thinks it is too late. Her moment
is over. It seems unfair that one should have only one moment.
It is so easy to miss it if one's head is even slightly turned. When
I leave the house in the evening I hear the child crying out for
me even if I put up the windows and race the motor. Once
when I was myself a child I wanted to save the whole world by
writing a book that would show everyone how wrong it was to be
prejudiced against any race or religion. And now all I wanted to
do was stop my child's weeping. A smaller task but still beyond
my grasp. The au pair would be fondling her boyfriend in the
garage and the child would be sleeping when I returned, but I

knew that I ought to have stayed home, I ought to have made a home, I ought not to leave a child who cried like that when I closed the door.

And so one day I was standing at the shore watching the child who was splashing in the froth. She was fearless and every few seconds needed to be pulled out of the way of the tide. She lay on her stomach and let the water wash over her and pull her small body out toward the great sea, and I would reach down and scoop her up, wet sand in her hair and her eyes, lumps of sand in the bathing-suit bottom, and she would hold me tightly around the neck and then again rush into the bubbling edge of the surf. And a man came and stood by my elbow.

His name was Norman Reiner. He was a doctor, a psychoanalyst. He had a house in Bridgehampton. He was friends with some painters and actors and he was on his August break. He thought I was the babysitter, not the mother. He was amused to find out I was not a babysitter. He asked me out for dinner. He was divorced and had his own children. There was salt in my hair and it was curly and wild and I smelled of suntan oil and zinc oxide for the child's nose and I thought, what can I offer a man like this. An older man, who couldn't possibly approve of the confusion that blew like desert sandstorms through my mind.

Actually I think at first it was not my mind he was interested in at all but the tufts of dark hair that stuck out of the top of my bikini and the beads of sweat that ran down the center line between my breasts and the smell of something I could never cover, a rankness that would not perfume away. We had dinner.

We had long conversations. He met the child. He did not think
the child was all right. We went to the movies. We went to
dinner with his friends. We went to a party with my friends. His
children came to visit. I met his children. He knew the artists
who lived in Springs. On his walls he had drawings and a
painting of flowers by a famous painter. He knew the daughter
of a famous acting teacher. He knew the famous acting teacher.
He knew poets. He was a doctor and a scientist and calm and
steady but he was not without a yearning for chaos and he
worked in the depths of the human mind where violence could
be transformed into images and hatreds roamed the streets like
stray cats in a bombed-out town on another continent.

I met a student of his and the student invited me out. This
was a psychoanalytic taboo. I liked both the teacher and the
student. I liked playing in the oedipal waters. That summer I
wore sundresses and talked about the Vietnam War and the
stories of Thomas Mann. That summer I put a flower behind my
ear when I went out to a party. And I wore shoes only on hot
pavements. That summer I could hear the au pair and her
boyfriend in rising pleasures all through the night. That summer
I wondered if I would ever love anyone again besides the child.
That summer I thought I must make the child happy. I must
stop her from screaming if I went into another room. I must find
out why she wakes in the middle of the night with such terrors
that her entire body shakes in my arms. One night, when I could
hardly calm her at all and great sobbing sounds were coming
from her small chest, I thought about the ocean and how I could
walk into it holding her in my arms and we would both be at

peace. And then I thought that I had better write something that could stand respectably next to Virginia Woolf before I imitated her death.

The nighttime sand flickered with the glowing lights of small worms that climbed in and out of invisible millimeter-wide holes along the shoreline. The nighttime moon on the sea would lead directly to my feet, a rising and falling shining road up and down the waves, coming to rest directly before my waiting body. The fog would come in and I would sit on the boardwalk and shiver. I knew Freud's question: What do women want? I didn't have the answer, at least not for this particular woman. Once at night I got a deep splinter in my foot and I had to go to the emergency room in Southampton to have it extracted and I limped about for a few days. Even Achilles had a vulnerable heel.

And so I was at a party on a lawn somewhere south of the highway, north of the pounding waves, when sitting on lawn chairs at some writer's home, a writer I admired so profoundly I could not speak a word in his presence, Dr. Norman Reiner confessed to me that despite the great affection he felt for me, I was not the one for him. His words came not as a blow but as a refreshing breeze. It was true. Whatever is meant by plighting one's troth, we could not plight to each other, not because we did not hold each other in deep regard but because the thing of insanity that makes for both trouble and excitement was missing between us. He was too sane at least on the surface and I was a knot of emotions that he knew would bind him in ways he did not wish to be bound. I also knew that I was Jewish and he,

although also Jewish, was looking for someone other, the
American dream, which could never be me. I came from
peddlers and tailors and so did he and I represented no
improvement at all. This seems shallow and offensive and in a
way it was, but on the other hand the emotions stirred by the
rankings of people in our society are raw and valid and the
piercings of pride take a long time to heal. Precisely because you
could mate with another social strata in America many longed
to do so. The papers showed photos of important men who were
of the upper class, they were diplomats, politicians, and they
belonged to clubs whose names the rest of us would not
recognize. The women's magazines showed models whose
beauty was Nordic and whose legs were long and whose hair was
straight and whose eyes were blue. I understood this. Anyone
who had read a novel by a Jewish male writer understood.
Passion is like a message on a vibration from outer space. It
arrives at its destination or it doesn't. Dr. Reiner and I were on
parallel planes. Also he thought the child would not be a good
addition to his days. She was not a good child. It would be rather
like bringing a demolition crew into his house, the child would
blaze and bang from wall to wall evermore. I understood. I had
loved Dr. Reiner but it was not right. I had loved Dr. Reiner but
it was not the kind of love that brings on the blues, that turns the
sky black, that makes a woman think that no one will ever be
right and she will be alone until death. That fall I went out with
a plump psychologist who was impotent and told me that he was
working on the problem with his therapist. I understood. Sex is
not as natural as it should be. He had a mother who was

depressed and a sister she preferred. He sent me flowers after each failed attempt and I could have stuffed several pillows with dead petals if I hadn't thrown the bouquets away.

AND THEN IT WAS December and I was soon to turn twenty-nine and I was invited to a party at Dr. Norman Reiner's apartment and I had a cold that turned my nose red and made my eyes squint and run. My throat was so sore, I could hardly speak. I should have stayed home. But I hired a babysitter and went out in the winter night bundled up in scarves and boots and carrying a bottle of aspirin in my bag. There were many people I knew at the party, a poet named Kenneth Koch, a writer who was writing about the Mob, and a few psychoanalysts all of whom had manuscripts that they wanted me to read. And then I saw a man smiling at another woman and the man's smile was the smile I wanted for myself. I wanted it because it was shy and soft and sweet and I wanted to be near the smile. I sneezed and sneezed and hoped I had sneezed myself out and went over to the man and I talked to him and he smiled at me and hope grasped my sore throat and made me shine, I know I was shining. I was also flirting as best as a woman with a very bad cold could flirt. He was a psychoanalyst too and his interest was in babies, their normal and abnormal growth, and he had worked with autistic children. He was divorced and had two daughters. And then someone else came over and then I melted away in the crowd. I had told him I was not married, that I had a child. I hoped he would call. I hoped I hadn't given him my cold.

I waited for his call and it didn't come. And by the time some weeks later I celebrated my thirtieth birthday with my child clinking her glass of milk against my white wine, I had given up.

1966: We have rented two houses in Amagansett. His is on the dunes and mine is farther away from the ocean. We have two young girls who will babysit for our children. The twelve-year-old is fretful but the eight-year-old is joyous with the beach, with Nancy Drew, with the lemonade stand she runs with my daughter. We have two houses because my soon-to-be husband doesn't want to confuse the children, wants us to be married before our households merge. I am amused. But I agree and in the early hours of the morning he returns to his place near the sea before his children wake. My child has no doubts as to why there are two dents in the pillows of the bed and why his wet bathing suit hangs on my line.

But then one very hot day with the sun high in the sky we go to the Artists and Writers baseball game. This is an annual event and it is talked about for days before and days afterward. The men who will play are not all athletes. Some are still a little confused about what is happening and when they should run and when they should stand still. Nevertheless it is always an epic ballgame and passions run high. We arrive a little late. The cars parked in the field are nestled one against the other like a herd of sheep. We find a spot and as we shut our car doors we hear a small faint cry, a whisper of a cry. It's a baby. But where is the baby? There are no other people in the parking lot. The game has begun, we can hear the cheers from the bleachers. I am carrying a bag with a thermos of iced tea. It is so hot that the backs of my legs have stuck to the leather of the automobile seat. It is so hot that the Queen Anne's lace at the edge of the road has withered. I don't want to miss any more of the game. Hurry, I say. But he stands there listening. It's a baby, he says. And so we follow the sound down one aisle of cars and up another and then the sound grows fainter. We have to find that baby, he says. And then we see her wrapped in a little pink blanket in the backseat of the car with the windows closed. The baby is white as a sheet. My husband-to-be in a few short months races to the bleachers and calls out, Who has a baby in a car? Get that baby out of the car, he shouts impolitely. He interrupts everyone's attention to the batter. The batter pauses. The pitcher puts his hands down to his sides. Everyone stares. Whose baby is it, the soon-to-be father of my young child roars. Someone rises. A woman with blond hair and sunglasses and a pout on her lips. She throws down her cigarette and stamps on it with the toe of her high-heeled shoe. Sweat is running down her legs.

She gets up and makes her way down to the ground and disappears. He follows her to her car and makes sure that the baby is breathing well enough. I wait for him in the parking lot. Neither of us want to see the game anymore. It was the Rivers's baby. It was one of his wives who had left her there, in the heat and the airless confines of the automobile. It was my doctor husband-to-be who said, "Murderous." "No," I said, "just careless."

1963–1964: New Year's eve I invited a few friends
over for breakfast after their parties. New Year's eve itself I spent
alone. I thought I was too old and had lost my moment. I was
worrying about my reproductive future.

Then I was invited to a great party at Tessa's. She was having
a belly dancer to celebrate her birthday. There would be a band
and caviar and champagne. I had a new dress to wear. I had
shoes that matched the dress. I wanted to see a belly dancer. But
a week before the party the man with the smile called to invite
me out to dinner the night of the party. It turned out that he had
thought I was Dr. Reiner's girlfriend and so he didn't call me,
thinking I was taken by his friend. But when he found out I was
available he called. He sounded shy on the phone. In fear that
he might not call back if I told him I was busy that night I
accepted. He came to the apartment to pick me up. The child
met him in the living room. They talked for a moment while I
gathered my things. The child walked us to the elevator door.
"Are you going to marry my mother?" she said. I was appalled.
"I don't know yet," he said. As the elevator door closed the child
started to scream.

We went to a movie. It was a sad movie about a Czech
woman taken off to Auschwitz. And afterward we had dinner at
an Italian restaurant and we talked and under the table he
touched my leg and over the table he smiled at me, that gentle
smile. He told me things about his childhood, about his love of
Trollope and how he had gone to a lecture on *Alice in
Wonderland* by a famous Viennese psychoanalyst and become

fascinated by Freud. He had grown up in Brooklyn and his first love was Ingrid Bergman, so blond and beautiful. But he seemed willing to linger at the table with me. I don't remember what I told him. When he brought me back to my door it was almost midnight. I said good night to him downstairs. I rode the elevator as if it were a racehorse. I changed into my party dress and my shoes and I took a taxi to Tessa's and the party was coming to an end when I arrived. There were empty glasses everywhere. A man was sleeping on the couch and at the bar, still drinking, was Jack. He was happy to see me. I was hoping to meet someone else but there was no one new to meet. A few hours later I was leaving and Jack was leaving too. We got into a cab together and when we arrived at my door he asked me for some money so he could take the cab downtown and continue his evening and I gave it to him, out of habit, out of sorrow.

1967 and on . . . : Several years after our divorce
Jack wrote a book on gambling and prostitutes and money, and it had its brilliant flashes but also a dirty mumbling side that made it seem almost beyond the pale just as the times were turning and war was upon us and sin was the least of our problems and the author seemed quite mad and the type who would never join the peace corps and people were having sex without guilt and guilt without sex and every other person was in EST trying to keep an emotional life from exploding and some were involved in primal scream and people were crawling through blue plastic tubes to find their inner infant and the

badness that was Jack, the badness that was gambling was just one of the points of darkness on a very dark night and Jack was doing things that were not so rare anymore or so romantic.

I waited for my date to call but not very long. He called the next evening and we went out again and again for about a month but he wouldn't sleep with me and I wondered if something was wrong with him too. Was he gay? Had he lost his penis in a tragic accident? Did he not find me desirable? And then one night in my living room while the child slept he explained he had been dating another woman novelist and he would have to break up with her before he could bed me.

1965–2010: He did and we began our life together, a life that lasted forty years.

I wonder if by passing my memories from the far corners of my neuron network to the pages that so effortlessly float onto my computer screen I am preserving them in typeset or I am emptying myself as a vessel would pour out the water into the waiting glass. I have seen dead bodies. They look as if they are compressed, shrunk, colorless. Is this writing project a sensible way to prepare for death or is it a doomed-to-fail attempt to relive, to remain, to undo mistakes, by judging them with the distance of time and experience? Years after the events in this book, when I was on a vacation trip to a dude ranch in the mountains of Colorado, I walked in a field of wildflowers. I plucked dozens of them from the earth and put each on a different page of a notebook, pressing them, drying them because I did not want to leave them behind when I returned home. When months later I opened that notebook I saw faint colors, a few dried stems, a leaf or two cracked and pale. I knew I should have left them where they were. They had their season.

And so we went to Hunter College and heard Anna Freud give a lecture to the gathered analysts and psychiatrists of New York City. I saw the little woman up on the stage, wearing a simple black dress. She was old now and not so strong but she carried the history of her time with her and the genius of her father followed her like a shadow and she spoke of the work of analysts to address the unknown within and I held on tight to the sleeve of my husband. Time was rustling in the hall. Don't ever forget this, not a moment, not a word, I told myself. If I had a bouquet of white roses in my arms I would have run up to the stage and placed them at Anna Freud's feet. As it was I tried to suppress tears that had no explanation.

And so I began to have dinner with analysts from Romania and Berlin who discussed papers they approved of and papers they disapproved of and trips they had taken to fine inns in far-flung corners of France and Italy and good wines and bad wines and I became an analyst's wife learning more and more about the web of id and ego and superego, defense and aggression, and I too wrote a book and one after that. Love was fine, but you needed work too. Freud said that. I believed him.

AND WHAT OF the child? She had a family: two half sisters and a stepsister. She had a dog and a cat and two hamsters. She knew all the words to *Hair*. She loved the Beatles and the

Rolling Stones. She went with us on long train rides to Washington, D.C., to protest the war. She went into rehab in a midwestern city, the same city where later Jack would also attempt to recover, and although they never met, they attended the same kind of meetings, protested the same belief in the same not so forgiving higher power, relapsed, recovered, and relapsed again. Her story is her own to tell. Its plot is still unfolding. She has a large rose tattoo on her back and sometimes when she forgets to take her AIDS medicine she has fevers. She reads her own poetry in cafés. She has published a book of short stories. She won several literary prizes. Sometimes she can write and sometimes she cannot.

Jack is safe inside the apartment he shares with his second wife. She works. They had a son. Jack loved his boy and his boy is fine. He had, I knew, a desire to be a kind and decent man, but that desire was, in earlier days, overwhelmed by the storms within.

Just before my second marriage Jack and I met in a hotel bar, one he chose. It was early, we were the only customers. There were mirrors on the walls and black-lacquered tables and gold sconces flickered dimly above us. It was his kind of place. It was always nighttime in there and the bartender was waiting for instructions. When I asked Jack to give the child up for adoption to my soon-to-be husband, he asked me about him, what he liked, what he did. I told him about his collection of George Eliot and the infant-development clinic he had started at Albert Einstein Medical College. I told him that he had loved the Dodgers and raged against their departure from Brooklyn. And then there was a softness in Jack's face. "He sounds like a good man," he said. "I wish I were that man." And I felt my heart flop in my chest. I felt his wish as if it were my wish to be a good woman. I felt like holding him in my arms. What comfort could I offer? I looked away. He signed the papers. Jack would have been a professor of Shakespeare or philosophy if his genes had allowed it. He would have written poetry to equal Auden's if only his desire for fame and fortune hadn't driven him half mad with the need for opiates of any brand. If only his synapses and neurons had been more obedient, a fraction quieter, a millimeter thicker. Instead he was a riverboat gambler who shot himself over and over again while swigging and snorting and dragging on his cigarette and charming the ladies and counting the cards and taking risks that ought not to be taken that left him sitting in hospital lounges wearing robes that were no doubt too short for his long legs.

I meet Carol Southern, long divorced from Terry, at a party on Fifth Avenue, the home of a musician and his painter wife. Carol and I look at each other. We shared memories that need not be spoken. "Do you regret it?" I say. "No," she says, "I loved every moment of it. I would do it again." She smiles her radiant and gentle smile. She is telling me the truth. I, on the other hand, would never do it again. Never.

Acknowledgments

I want to thank my editor, Nan Talese, who understands it all.

I am grateful to my agent, Lisa Bankoff, who has been a friend throughout the years.

My work would not be my work and my life would not be my life without my family, all of whom have helped me endure.

A Note About the Author

Anne Roiphe's eighteen books include the memoir
Fruitful, a finalist for the National Book Award, and the
novel *Up the Sandbox*, a national best seller. She has written
for *The New York Times*, *The New York Observer*, *Vogue*, *Elle*,
Redbook, *Parents*, and *The Guardian*, and is a contributing
editor to *The Jerusalem Report*. She lives in New York City.

A Note About the Type

The text of this book was set in Electra, a typeface designed by W. A. Dwiggins (1880–1956). This face cannot be classified as either modern or old style. It is not based on any historical model, nor does it echo any particular period or style. It avoids the extreme contrasts between thick and thin elements that mark most modern faces, and it attempts to give a feeling of fluidity, power, and speed.

3